CORONA VIRUS, INFECTIOUS DISEASES & ECONOMIC CRISIS RECOVERY

Copyright © 2020 by Doron Benbenisty

All rights reserved. No part of this book may be reproduced or transmitted in any form or by any means without written permission from the author.

Printed in USA by AMAZON

DEDICATION

First dedication is with the loving memory of Ron Minnino, the first CRI instructor in Las Vegas, a dear friend, and colleague. We are missing you very much. May you find rest and peace, in heaven.

Ron Minnino is on the far right

The second dedication is for all the first responders and medical teams all over the world that are risking their lives on behalf of helping others. "The second time in the field of human conflict and crisis was so much owed by so many to so few." Sir Winston Churchill and Doron Benbenisty

DISCLAIMER

This book details the author's personal experiences and his theories ,his will to try to help, provide out-of-the-box solutions with opinions about the Coronavirus, infectious diseases defense, and economic crisis recovery. The author and/or his company/companies are not a healthcare provider. The author and publisher are providing this book and its contents on an "as is" basis and make no representations or warranties of any kind with respect to this book or its contents. The author and publisher disclaim all such representations and warranties, including for example warranties of merchantability and healthcare for a particular purpose. In addition, the author and publisher do not represent or warrant that the information accessible via this book is accurate, complete, or current. The statements made about products and services have not been evaluated by the U.S. Food and Drug Administration. They are not intended to diagnose, treat, cure, or prevent any condition or disease. Please consult with your own physician or healthcare specialist regarding the suggestions and recommendations made in this book. Except as specifically stated in this book, neither the author or publisher, nor any authors, contributors, or Other representatives will be liable for damages arising out of or in connection with the use of this book. This is a comprehensive limitation of liability that applies to all damages of any kind, including (without limitation) compensatory; direct, indirect or consequential damages; loss of data, income or profit; loss of or damage to property and claims of third parties. You understand that this book is not intended as a substitute for consultation with a licensed healthcare practitioner, such as your physician. Before you begin any healthcare program or change your lifestyle in any way, you will consult your physician or another licensed healthcare practitioner to ensure that you are in good health and that the examples contained in this book will not harm you. This book provides content related to physical and/or mental health issues. As such, use of this book implies your acceptance of this disclaimer.

TABLE OF CONTENTS

Dedication 2

Preface 6

Introduction 7

Chapter 1 - What Is The Difference.... 11

Chapter 2 - Quick Reference Guide.. 14

Chapter 3 - The Most Common Surfaces 20

Chapter 4 - How To Reduce The Chance 24

Chapter 5 - Does Facial Hair Increase.................................... 28

Chapter 6 - Tools And Equipment 30

Chapter 7- Have A Pet Like A Dog 37

Chapter 8 - Prepare and Stock Up... 39

Chapter 9 - How To Test For Coronavirus 41

Chapter 10 - Children Can Contract The Coronavirus 47

Chapter 11- How To Guide Your Child.................................. 50

Chapter 12 - Safety Protocols 55

Chapter 13 - You Lose Your Job Due To 77

Chapter 14- Joint Venture Brokering...................................... 81

Chapter 15- Working From Home 86

Chapter 16- Starting A New Business..................................... 95

Chapter 17 - The Deep Side Of Marketing.............................100

Chapter 18 - Digital Marketer Profession...............................104

Chapter 19 - Medical Rescue At 30,000 Feet.........................106

Chapter 20-Conclusion And Resources.................................. 110

Visit the website: https://www.helpmebesafe.com/ for free videos, the above product and additional product that my company and I have developed.

PREFACE

while the world is struggling to cope with the coronavirus epidemic and world economic crisis, my company I decided to create a comprehensive solution that will help with educating the world on how to better defend against the COVID-19 and other infectious diseases. This book is the first part of a three-part solution that I and my company offer:
1. This book
2. The video training portal
3. Consultation

I'm hoping that you will find the knowledge in this book beneficial and that you are going to implement the information taught in this book. Also, I invite you to the online video training portal, where you can watch a comprehensive training video course.

Last, I am available as an advisor on the coronavirus, defensive protocols, and implementation of out-of-the-box solutions to various industries verticals. My consultation services are available for both small and large groups, as well as government agencies, corporations, and countries.

INTRODUCTION

While countries and their governments are putting tremendous effort into containing the Coronavirus (Novel Coronavirus, COVID-19), it seems like this virus is fast becoming a world pandemic. In the history of the world, there has never been a virus or disease that has spread so rapidly across the entire globe. During the last Ebola virus outbreak in Africa, the African people suffered severely with many dying. By contrast, the Coronavirus is a worldwide pandemic that spreads regardless of race, sex, or place of residency.

Many so-called experts are saying that you shouldn't worry and that the virus is more like the regular flu in most cases. I disagree with this assumption and find it very biased. They say that the majority of Coronavirus fatalities are older people with pre-existing conditions and, if you are a healthy person, that you shouldn't worry. This is not the correct approach. In various hospitals all over the world, there are people right now who were young and completely healthy without pre- existing medical conditions who have contracted it. These people are now connected to life support systems; some are being put into induced comas and are fighting to stay alive. This is why each person must do whatever he or she can in order to take the proper steps to avoid becoming infected by the Coronavirus, as well as any other infectious diseases.

In this book, I will share special knowledge, skills, and protocols that will enable you to overcome fear, uncertainty and to equip yourself with potentially life-saving knowledge that will allow you to better protect yourself and your loved ones.

This book is divided into six parts:
1. The Coronavirus, infectious diseases and how to avoid infection
2. Strategic planning in case you become infected with the Coronavirus
3. Strategic preparation for curfews, sheltering In place, mandatory isolation and self-confinement
4. Useful day-to-day protocols
5. Risk and vulnerability assessments
6. Conclusions and resources

A lot has been discussed about the recent outbreak of the Novel Coronavirus. Since there is a lot of misinformation and rumors, it's easy to get confused. I hope to clear up all the myths and present you with accurate information.

So, let's start with first learning more about this virus.

What is Coronavirus?

Coronavirus is actually a larger family of viruses that cause illnesses such as the common cold, severe acute respiratory syndrome (SARS) and the Middle East respiratory syndrome (MERS). A new outbreak of the Coronavirus erupted in 2019 in China. Though the general consensus is that the official approx. size of Novel Coronavirus is 120nm in diameter (Britannica.com), my research has uncovered that some
particles and bits of the Novel Coronavirus can be as small as 20nm.

Some other names attributed to the Coronavirus are severe acute respiratory syndrome Corona virus 2 (SARS-CoV-2) and the Corona-virus disease 2019 (COVID-19).

Coronavirus affects both animals and humans. There can be cases where the virus infected animals and turned into a new virus that infected humans. These mutations are more lethal forms of Coronavirus since they can lead to pneumonia, which can be life-threatening.

The three most common illnesses resulting from the virus are:

- SARS (severe acute respiratory syndrome) – It's a fatal respiratory illness discovered in China in 2002. There haven't been any new cases reported under this virus since 2002.

- MERS (Middle East respiratory syndrome) – This severe respiratory illness was first reported in Saudi Arabia in 2012. From there, it spread to 27 countries, including the USA, where two cases were reported. All cases were discovered to have their source in the Arabian Peninsula.

- COVID-19 (Coronavirus disease 2019) – Erupting in Wuhan City in 2019, the source has been found to originate from the Hubei Province. Since then, the disease has spread to most countries around the world, with a high number of cases and deaths reported in the USA. All updates with regards to the disease are being monitored by the Centers for Disease Control (CDC) and the World Health Organization (WHO).

What are the Symptoms of Coronavirus?

Originally the symptoms of the Novel Coronavirus arise when people travelled to or from areas of the outbreak of the virus or have been in contact with anyone travelling from those areas. Today it's so widespread that you can contract the virus just about anywhere, by coming into contact with someone who has it or has come into contact with a contaminated surface without taking the proper safety measures.

The symptoms of Coronavirus infections in general are:
- Fever
- Cough
- Shortness of breath
- Sore throat
- Headache

The specific symptoms of COVID-19 are:
- Fever
- Cough
- Shortness of breath

The symptoms of COVID-19 have been found to be milder than the ones for SARS and MERS. In some cases, if you haven't traveled to these infected areas or you haven't had contact with anyone from these areas, then the symptoms may just be of another virus like the flu. However, as we are witnessing new developments in many countries, Coronavirus is becoming one of the worst world pandemics to have infected millions.

CHAPTER ONE

WHAT IS THE DIFFERENCE BETWEEN A VIRUS AND A BACTERIUM?

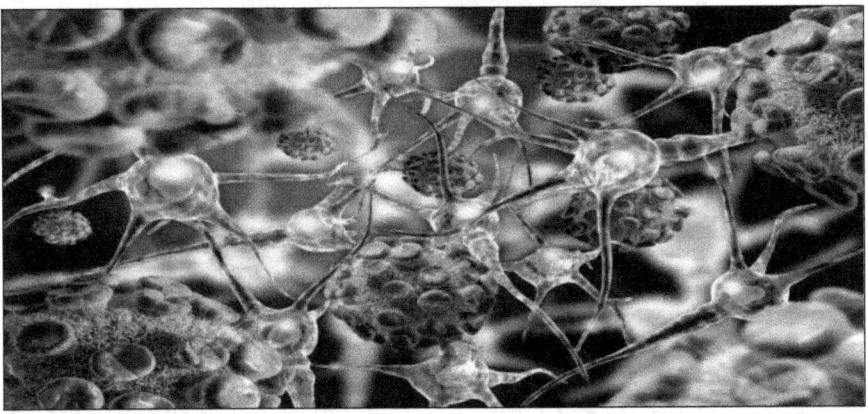

For many, it is hard to distinguish between bacteria and a virus. So, what's the difference between a virus and a bacterium? Why antibiotics cannot cure the Novel Coronavirus?

The Novel Coronavirus has caused more infection than Ebola and more deaths than SARS. For years there hasn't been a virus that has caused such a rapid infection of so many people. This rapid and violent outbreak has caused severe panic around the world, even in the medical world. The number of victims is stunning.

What exactly is the Coronavirus? Is it different from bacteria or other viruses, and why aren't antibiotics effective against it?

It is essential to mention that the Coronavirus is unlike a bacterium in that bacteria are dependent on other living cells to reproduce. Outside of the bodies that host it, a virus is inactive. Only after it penetrates the cell and acclimates within it can it reproduce. The hereditary material among viruses is partial, and also, they are unable to move on their own. Hence, a virus's mobility depends on it being resourceful by moving on or within things like floating in the air or flowing in body fluids.

In fact, the Novel Coronavirus infection occurs when it travels in disbursed body fluids like saliva from one person to another. The micro particles are inhaled through the nose or mouth and reach the lungs. The virus begins to bind to infected cells, penetrate the cells, and utilize the DNA of the host cell to replicate in large quantities. The newly created viruses exit the cell and begin to infect more cells.

Unlike bacteria, which cause diseases requiring antibiotic treatment, viruses usually cause a mild illness, which passes within a few days without any treatment. In the case of the Coronavirus, most infected people recover from the disease, which is expressed differently than a bacterial illness.

Different disease symptoms between bacteria and virus infections:
Viruses usually cause secretions from the nose, ears, and /or eyes and are transparent. This is unlike bacteria, which causes a green or murky secretion.

- Virally infected experience watery diarrhea, as opposed to mucosal diarrhea caused by bacteria.
- With viral infections, coughs are usually accompanied by a runny nose and fever above 39 degrees.
- Viruses will cause macular rashes which disappear upon gentle pressure against the skin and then reappear upon releasing that pressure, as opposed to bacterial rashes, which cause visible dots and remain constantly visible when applying gentle pressure and also while releasing it.

Antibiotic drugs work differently on bacterial cells, as opposed to the way they work on viruses. When given unnecessarily, antibiotics can cause the formation of drug-resistant bacteria. Its resistance can get so extreme that it could cause hospitalization and the need for more specific effective antibiotics. Some doctors and specialists have been experimenting with introducing the antibodies produced by people who had the Coronavirus into the blood of critically ill patients to test the potential of building immunity.

Source: https://inside.mountsinai.org/blog/mount-sinai-to-begin-the-transfer-of-covid-19-antibodies-into-critically-ill-patients/

Still, there are a few antiviral drugs that manage to inhibit virus replication. These include anti-herpes, hepatitis, HIV, and anti-influenza drugs. The few antiviral drugs that have been developed are specifically designed for particular viruses, as opposed to antibiotics that can work against a vast range of bacteria.

The most effective way to combat virus infection is through vaccines. Vaccines have been able to aid in the extermination of diseases such as smallpox, significantly reduced complications from viruses such as Rota, reduced the rate of hepatitis A infection, and reduced complications and morbidity from other many other viruses. At the time of writing this book, scientists have been able to utilize genetic mapping to complete a three-dimensional structure of the Coronavirus. These steps are extremely significant towards effective drug and vaccination development. However, even among the most optimistic forecasts, vaccination completion is unlikely to happen within this year. However as the author of this book it's my belief that more important than the vaccine is the development of a medicine and a cure for people that have bad or severe reaction to the coronavirus. Furthermore, While most of the population will develop a natural immunity to the virus, a vaccine can come at a second phase can be implemented to increase the immunity of people in high risk condition.

CHAPTER TWO

COMMON QUESTIONS AND ANSWERS ABOUT THE CORONAVIRUS QUICK REFERENCE GUIDE

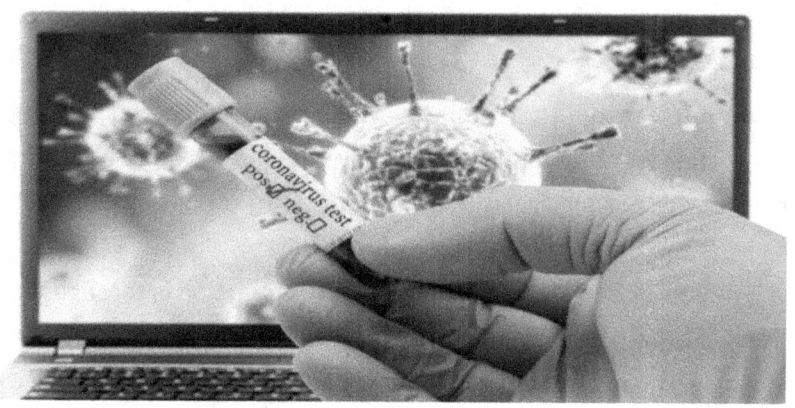

1. How do you get the virus?

Today it is known that the virus can be transmitted between humans less than 1-2 meters (approx. 6ft) apart and within exposure after 15 minutes. You will know if you are too close - if you can smell the breath of the person. This means that as he speaks, shrapnel/particles from his mouth may reach you. In addition, the virus is probably being transmitted by contact with surfaces. Therefore, you should avoid your contaminated hands coming in contact with your eyes, nose, or mouth.

2. Does the virus also pass through animals?

This possibility is not yet confirmed, although some different strands of Coronavirus have been discovered in some animals like camels, cats, tigers, cattle and bats. It appeared that human can infect animals with the coronavirus however not the other way. This issue is still under investigation.

3. Does the virus pass through an insect bite?

At the moment, this does not seem to be the case, as it is found that the virus mainly passes on from saliva that penetrates the respiratory system, and not through the blood. However, this issue is still under investigation.

4. Can this virus be caught by traveling on a bus or train?

Yes. However, it is advisable to practice safe hygiene protocols such as wearing masks, protect the eyes, and disinfect hands at the end of the journey and not to touch your eyes, nose or mouth with your hands. Where possible, it is best to sit at an open window for increased air circulation. If someone next to you coughs or sneezes, immediately hold your breath and quickly distanced yourself from that person as far as you can.

5. Can the virus pass through sex?

There is currently no evidence that the virus is transmitted through having sex. However, the Coronavirus can certainly be passed on through the swapping of saliva by kissing, coughing, sneezing, spitting, or touching open areas of your body like your eyes, nose, or mouth with contaminated hands.

6. **How should you act in isolation?** Stay in a separate, well-ventilated room with a closed door, do not go to public spaces, do not go to work or to educational institutions, and do not use public transport. If you are suspicious of infection do not go directly to clinics or hospitals, call EMS so they can take the right precautions to get you treatment without infecting others.
7. Also, in the United States, the CDC has a help line.

8. Should I start walking around public areas and sidewalks with a mask on?

Face masks do not prevent adhesion of saliva particles. This is because the tightest and most elaborate mask, N95, does not prevent particle penetration of less than 0.3 microns. The estimated Coronavirus size is 0.1 micron, more specifically about 120nm in diameter. Meanwhile, the mask did not reduce the rate of infection in China. It is also important to remember that the main infectious contract is through sneezing and coughing, and this occurs most often when a person wearing a mask removes it to cough or sneeze.

9. How to prevent Coronavirus infection?

Practice safe hygiene rules, which include coughing or sneezing on the cuff or elbow and not on or in the palm of your hand. Avoid nail- biting, rubbing your eyes or nose, avoid your hands touching public surfaces, and keeping infected persons humanely isolated and safe. It is crucial to maintain good hand hygiene, and that includes soaking them in water and washing with soap for at least 60 seconds several times a day or disinfecting them with alcohol gel.

10. How do you get the Coronavirus?

The virus mainly passes through the spread of saliva that enters the respiratory system, which means most likely it is present and can be passed on through the spread of tears or other body secretions, including feces.

11. Who does the virus attack most?

The infection data shows that the Coronavirus rarely hits children under nine. Most of the severely ill are adults, especially those with a history of background illnesses such as diabetes, asthma, obesity, heart disease, and immunosuppressants. Lately, cases of children and young adults 1-35 have been increasing due to their lack of social retention during festivals, parties, and outings.

12. Can Coronavirus be contracted from eating food prepared by a carrier or in a carrier's environment?

Indeed, there is potential for infection from both the use of shared tools and from food prepared by a bearer of the disease. Coronavirus passes through splinters. However, it is still unclear whether or not ingested infected food survives gastric acidity.

13. Should you plan flights this summer or later?

The eruption and spread of the Coronavirus are not expected to disappear within the next few months. Therefore, it is advisable at this stage to avoid non-essential booking flights.

14. How is the adhesive test performed in Coronavirus?

Coronavirus detection is performed by the extraction of a sample taken from the nose or throat using a marker that is delivered to a laboratory for assay testing. This is where the specimen is placed in vitro by means of a technique called PCR (Polymerase chain reaction). It is used to amplify trace amounts of DNA or RNA in or on any liquid/surface. The specimen is heated and cooled many times. Along with the presence of a bacterium, the viral material section is cut and duplicated and is compared to the Coronavirus. The result is obtained within about 5 hours. In some cases, more invasive respiratory testing has to be conducted with intubation of the respiratory tract when sufficient samples can't be obtained via standard tests.

15. What is the origin of the Coronavirus?

The latest strand of Coronavirus originated in Wuhan, China. It is also known as the 2019-NCov scientific name belongs to the Coronavirus family. This sub-strain is the seventh in a family of sub-strains, known to infect humans. It is estimated that new viruses are created over the years of mutations, which are genetic changes that make viruses more resistant and violent. The name of the Coronavirus, like the other viruses in this group, is given to it because of the "crown" shape it forms as a result of various protein receptors on its mantle, which help it enter other live cells.

16. What are the symptoms of Coronavirus patients?

The disease usually manifests mild and transient flu-like symptoms, which include headache, weakness, runny nose, sore throat or cough, and muscle pain. In some cases, the disease will also be accompanied by complications that include high fever, difficulty breathing, pneumonia, and sometimes even blood and death infection.

17. How are patients treated?

Potential patients who have been living in infected areas in China and those who may be experiencing the symptoms of a severe illness, within 14 days of staying there, are considered potential carriers. Such a patient is placed in isolation, and laboratory tests are performed that include swabbing the mouth or nose to retrieve a sample for detection of the Coronavirus. Since antibiotics do not work against this virus, there is currently no treatment for the disease other than supportive assistance that includes medical supervision and fluid delivery. In case of respiratory deterioration, patients are given prophylactic antibiotics and assistive respiratory system support.

18. Why is the novel Coronavirus vaccine production delayed? There
are several companies that have already started the process
of creating the vaccine, but this is a project that may take months and potentially the collaboration of many medical entities or even countries. To create a vaccine, it is necessary to extract some of the virus's antibodies from infected people. This is necessary to isolate sections of the virus's hereditary material, RNA, for analysis. Scientists are trying to

combine several key factors to come up with a vaccine by identifying protein structures that have helped in preventing or blocking the virus's ability to infiltrate, bind to, enter cells, impede multiplication, increase resiliency and boost the body's immune capabilities. They have to multiply the virus in large enough quantities in order to culture it for quantitative testing. Whatever the method, it is a long-term production that, even if accelerated, may take up to two years or more.

19. How to get back home after traveling from abroad in an infected Coronavirus environment?

It is desirable for a family member to pick you up in a private vehicle. If there is no other option, return home by taxi. However, though you may have the virus without showing any symptoms, you are still contagious. This is why you should stay away from other people. If you have to be in the presence of other uninfected people due solely to circumstance, do the decent thing by taking the necessary steps to prevent transmission by following the safety protocols and taking precautions. There is no way to know how someone else's body will cope with contracting the Coronavirus from you, so if you have it, do the right thing!

CHAPTER THREE

THE MOST COMMON SURFACES AND OBJECTS FOR CONTRACTING THE CORONAVIRUS

While the CDC and the World Health Organization are doing their best to educate us on how to protect ourselves from contracting the Coronavirus, it's important to note that there are several surfaces and objects that are good at disguising microorganisms that could be extremely contagious. Many of us forget that we need to constantly disinfect those surfaces, instruments and products for bacteria, fungus and viruses, especially the new extremely contagious novel Coronavirus.

What we have learned from studying the Coronavirus situation in China is that there are many cases where the virus has survived in some instances for up to 17 days on some surfaces. As previously stated, the virus can survive while suspended in the air for up to 3 hours (in case that there is isn't any airflow such as an open window or a door) up to 4 hours on copper, up to 24 hours on cardboard and even up to 3 days on plastic and stainless steel. The following are arguably the most popular potentially contagious surfaces:

Smartphones

As you will see and learn in a separate chapter, cell phones, and smartphones can be extremely dirty and have potentially contagious surfaces.

Door handles and handrails

Arguably the most commonly used surfaces in both buildings and vehicles; try not to touch them with your bare hands. Use gloves and/or use your elbow or foot when possible to open doors. On handrails, again, you can use gloves or support your body with your elbow. It is important not to touch your face with your hands and also to disinfect your hands and the parts of your clothing that have been in contact with the door handles and other potentially infected surfaces.

Light switches, buttons, remote controls, ATM machines, and keypads

It is hard to believe how many potentially contagious hands touch various buttons and keypads daily. This is why it's so important not to touch your face. Wear gloves when possible. Use a pen, stick, or a pointed object to press buttons. Always carry with you a 70% alcohol- concentrate in a spray bottle.

Fuel/gas pump, electrical car charging stations

As mentioned, at the beginning of the book, you read how potentially contaminated gas pump refueling handles, or car charging plugs are. This is why it's important to follow the protocols practiced in the videos included in this book.

Keyboard and mouse

Offices that share computers, notepads, iPads, and tablet PCs can be a potentially contagious source for viruses and bacteria. It's important to disinfect every working station each time you sit down and get up and walk away from it. Alcohol wipes should be used. However, it's important after that to wash or wipe with water when possible all surfaces in order to prevent the alcohol from potentially damaging the electronics.

Shoes and shoelaces

Almost no one thinks about how dirty the bottom of our shoes must be. When we walk in our shoes daily, we are stepping on extremely dirty surfaces including bacteria, funguses, viruses, etc. Have you ever stopped to think and consider when I'm taking off my shoes; do I touch the bottom of the shoes or the heel? What if I don't touch the sole or heel of my shoe but just the top body part, is that dirty as well? Or after touching the bottom of my shoe, do I go and wash or disinfect my hands?

After asking several people of various ages, I discovered that none of them really think about it. Many of them touch these shoe parts, in one way or another, without considering if they should disinfect their hands. It's important to disinfect the bottom of your shoes with alcohol wipes and other types of disinfection products that could be friendly to the shoe and shoelace materials. I believe that just by reading this paragraph and implementing it, you could reduce the chance of contracting the virus by hundreds of percent.

Children's' playgrounds and toys

One thing that always keeps parents worried is the possibility of their child contracting an illness or becoming contaminated with bacteria or a virus while playing at the playground, or playing with other children's toys. During the flu season and especially during a world crisis like the Coronavirus pandemic, I advise parents to try to prevent taking their children to a public playground and or to other children's houses to play.

It is tough to enforce limited mobility on children or to restrict them from touching their faces, especially the younger ones. As a rule of thumb, the minute you take your kids back to your car, just before you let them into the car, you must disinfect their hands with 70% alcohol wipes or any other disinfecting product. Also, try to minimize the interaction of your child with other potentially sick children.

Fitness gym and martial art studios

Although it is the responsibility of the gym manager or martial arts instructor to make sure no one who is contagious or sick is utilizing the facility. However, you must always beware of those around you and protect yourself from infection and contamination. It is still up to you to be responsible and considerate with respect to yourself and others. If you are not feeling well, you shouldn't go to any populated public place until you are sure you are longer contagious.

If you must go out in public, wear a face mask and gloves. Make sure besides taking water and towel, you also take alcohol spray, wipes, or some type of other disinfecting agents. Try to confirm that you're disinfecting agent is allowed to be used on the various surfaces and instruments where you are going. The most important thing is not to touch your face, which is extremely difficult to do when you are sweating and wiping your forehead or face. Make sure before you get into your car to disinfect your hands or alternatively use gloves throughout the process.

Restaurants, fast-food establishments, malls and food courts, credit cards

Think of how many people got food poisoning or the stomach flu after dining outside of their home. This alone should give you an idea of how potentially contagious tables, menus, utensils, napkins, etc. are. We produced a comprehensive video course that explains the safety protocol that we are recommending.

CHAPTER FOUR

HOW TO REDUCE THE CHANCE OF CONTRACTING THE CORONAVIRUS [COVID-19]

Some people believe there isn't much they can do to prevent contracting a virus, but I disagree. Having a good immune system is your first line of defense, as well as a decent insurance policy that will afford you meds and treatment in case you do contract the virus. As of this writing, there is no vaccine or definite remedy to overcome the Coronavirus. This is why it's so important to have a robust immune system to fight the virus effectively. The safety practices in this book are designed to help decrease your chance of not contracting the virus. Later on, in this book, I will tell you several ways to boost and strengthen your immune system.

Some of the most basic ways to avoid contracting the virus are to avoid touching the face or your head, as well as proper handwashing protocols. You should wash your hands frequently with hot water and soap for at least 60 seconds. If you are not able to wash them, then the use of alcohol/disinfecting gel or wipes with at least 70% alcohol is suggested. Getting into the habit of washing your hands before you leave home and then washing them once you return is ideal.

Let me give you some examples of how you would deal with an everyday situation such as pumping gas. You have three options, all according to where you live:

Option 1 – You stop your vehicle, and there is a serviceman or a woman to refuel your car. All you need to do is give them your debit or credit card.

Option 2 – You walk inside the gas station, and you prepay for gas at the counter, either with cash or debit/credit card.

Option 3 – You stop your vehicle, get out of the car, put your card into the machine, insert your card code, maybe you need to press on an LCD screen to select the fuel options and pump your own gas.

All the options that I just described in Options 1, 2, and 3 require different actions.

In **Option 1**, the responsible thing to do would be first to disinfect your hands using alcohol gel or wipes. Then reach for your wallet or purse, take out the cash or debit/credit card and hand it to the service person. Once the refueling is done, you'll get your card back; sometimes, you may need to sign payment verification. If you need to sign anything with a regular pen, make sure to use your own pen. If you must use a digital pen, disinfect your hands afterward. Be sure to accept the card with only two fingers to minimize exposure. Disinfect your hands and your card again with alcohol-based/disinfecting gel or wipes, ensuring you clean your two fingers thoroughly. Only return your card to your wallet or purse after you've disinfected the card and your hands. During this time, do not touch your face, hair, or rub your ears, eyes, mouth, or nose.

In **Option 2 and 3**, you will need to walk inside the store to pay with cash or card. If you are using cash, be mindful of the safety of others, and thoroughly disinfect your hands before leaving your vehicle. When paying with cash, put the cash into a Ziploc/plastic bag to pay to the person behind the counter. Then ask them to put the change inside your Ziploc bag while you are holding it open for them. Then close it. In this case, it's good to have disinfecting/alcohol-based spray, wipes or gel that you can carry on you. If you are paying with a card, it is good to have a designated pen or something similar that you can sign with. Use the pen tip to press on the card machine panel after you insert your card. Then if you need to sign, use the pen to sign. At this point, when you take the merchandise or the receipt, do not touch your face or your head. Sanitize your hands after the transaction for good measure to avoid cross-contamination.

When you return to your car to refuel, remove the fuel handle. Select the fuel type and start refueling your vehicle. When you finish, return the handle. Before you touch your vehicle door, make sure you disinfect your hands with disinfecting/alcohol-based gel, spray or wipes of 70% alcohol. When you get home or to your destination, if you bought anything from the store, be sure to disinfect the merchandise, for example, energy drinks or water bottles, etc. before touching or consuming them. As for the Ziploc/plastic bag containing your change, at the end of the day, spray the money (bills and coins) with alcohol- based spray and then remove them from the bag.

I know it may seem like a laborious procedure, but if you put your mind to it, you can do it as an example of why this precaution is necessary. The customer before you may have been an infected person who just fueled their vehicle, sneezed or coughed into their hand, used their card to pay, pressed the buttons on the keypad, and then touched the refueling handle while refueling. However, that person may not have shown signs of an active Coronavirus carrier; they may indeed be unknowingly infected with the virus. Now, although you never came into direct contact with him/her physically, you have unknowingly increased your chances of contracting the virus by thousands of percent unnecessarily. This is why you are not only risking yourself but all the other people that you will come into contact with, including your loved ones. Teach them these procedures and advise them to be careful to avoid becoming infected and contagious to the rest of the family.

Social Distancing

When greeting others in some cultures, the custom is not to touch the other person. For example, in some Asian cultures, it is respectful to bow instead. The West, however, is a far more physical culture, both in business and social gatherings. Handshakes, kisses, hugs, or tapping on someone's shoulder should be avoided altogether. Before anyone extends a hand to you, simply say: "I apologize, but because of the Coronavirus, for both of our sakes, we should avoid touching each other. Let's use the Asian way of a simple, respectful bow." During social gatherings, try to keep at least 6 feet away from a person with whom you are speaking. You may not know it, but whenever a person speaks, tiny microscopic droplets of saliva spread from his or her mouth in unseen mists, and that is why it's crucial to keep a responsible distance during communication and interaction.

There are many other social setups such as the workplace, schools, movie theaters, trains or subways, commercial flights, supermarkets, restaurants, etc. In these and many others, I will talk specifically about various behavioral safety protocols that you can practice in order to reduce the likelihood of contracting the Coronavirus.

CHAPTER FIVE

DO YOU HAVE STUBBLE OR BEARD? DOES FACIAL HAIR INCREASE THE RISK OF CONTRACTING AND BECOMING INFECTED WITH CORONAVIRUS?

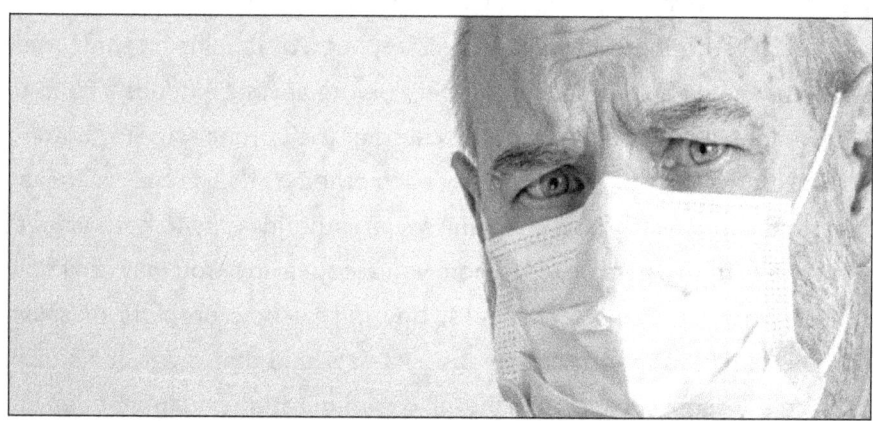

Nowadays, the best practice is to be clean-shaven, lowering the probability of contracting the virus. The American Disease Control Center is warning people with stubble or beards about possible infection with the Coronavirus. The reason: Facial hair impedes the mask's seal around the face, thereby allowing small particles occupying small pieces of saliva to enter the respiratory system via penetrating the spaces created between the mask and the face. These are the types of elders who are at the highest risk of contracting the virus through improperly sealing masks.

The CDC has created a table for all types of beards, mustaches, and bristles that are currently recommended and indicating those that will prevent good sealing. The most normal look for face mask wearers, of course, is clean-shaven. Other good facial arrangements include a mustache called a "Nazi inverted" jar, which is perpendicular to the lower lip of the mouth, wigs up to half the face. Mustaches above the upper lip and mustaches that do not extend beyond the face compound are not recommended. All other mustaches and beards are unadvisable, and their wearers increase the risk of becoming infected.

Now the question is - do masks lead to a decrease in the infection rate?

From what has been learned so far, the answer is not absolute. It turns out that most of the reported infections occurred when maskers who wore them removed them, sneezed, and put them back on, causing the sneezes or coughs to spread contaminated saliva throughout the air. In hindsight, the Chinese have been wearing masks for about a month, and the Coronavirus distribution rate there was one of the highest in the world. However, if there is no better protection, it is likely that wearing a mask provides a basic defense in any event.

Another concern is that the Coronavirus may also infect the lining of the eyes, which no mask promises to prevent. Surface contact can also cause infection. It is feared that touching your fingers on a surface infected with the Coronavirus is one of the leading causes of infection. This virus is likely to survive for up to 9 days outside the body and can cause infection. As a rule of thumb, if you are wearing a mask, make sure you protect your eyes as well with eye protection glasses that can cover your eyes not just from the front but from the sides as well. If you are wearing eyeglasses daily, you can get large protective goggles that can cover the top of your eyeglasses or you can modify your glasses if need be, by adding a piece of nonporous material to prevent the accessibility to your eyes by particles accessing your eyes from the side.

CHAPTER SIX

INFECTIOUS DISEASE TOOLS AND EQUIPMENT

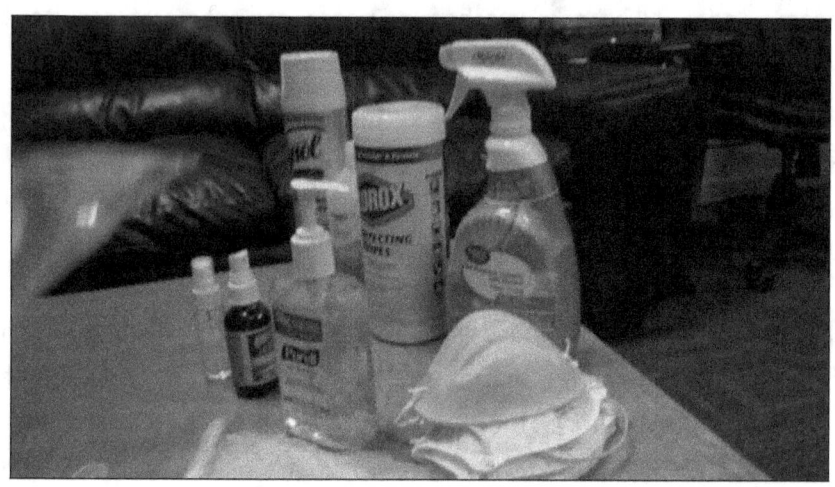

MASKS: ARE MASKS EFFECTIVE AGAINST THE CORONAVIRUS?

As many of us know, China was the first to start having to deal with the Novel Coronavirus. One of the first things the Chinese government put into place was a mandatory mask-wearing policy. Unfortunately, even with this mandatory policy, the epidemic still expanded rapidly. Different masks protect differently, but many people were removing their masks when they coughed, therefore defeating the mask's purpose.

Do I recommend not wearing a mask? Negative. While many experts say that masks will not help protect you from the Coronavirus because the virus is so small. A mask can still act as a barrier to help prevent you from spreading it to others. It can also assist you in trying to prevent getting sick from other viruses and infections. While the Coronavirus is spreading, there are still other diseases and sicknesses lurking around, and your goal should be to avoid getting sick from any pathogens. Even the common cold or a sinus infection can compromise your immune system and make you more vulnerable to the Coronavirus. There are multiple fungi and bacteria type viruses and diseases that can still weaken your immune system. In addition to this, a mask can help remind you not to touch your face. These are some of the reasons why I recommend wearing a mask when you are around people.

WHICH TYPE MASK SHOULD I CHOOSE?

The exact size of the Coronavirus is still unknown. But "its" cousin, the SARS virus that caused a mass outbreak in 2003, is tiny, with a diameter of 0.1 microns. The tightest mask is capable of blocking fragments up to 0.3 microns in size, at least theoretically. The Coronavirus can pass through those openings.

THE SIMPLE MASK

There are several types of face masks on the market: the simplest is a mask that covers the mouth, which is worn with rubber wrapped around the ear. This mask is not at all immune to infection, as the nose remains exposed enough for the Coronavirus to still potentially enter the body.

THE SURGICAL MASK

A tighter fit less penetrable mask is the surgical mask. It is the same mask or similar to the masks used by operating room teams. However, the "version" that is sold to most people, includes elastic bands around the ears. This mask is "loose", not tight enough and can allow small particles to penetrate from the sides and upper direction of the face. Given this information, the surgical mask is not tight enough. A more "professional" mask is also used by operating room medical teams. This mask covers both the nose and the mouth, with two pairs of laces tied at the back of the neck. This mask, too, is not tightly sealed and is not considered to be totally protective against viruses.

N95/N99 MASK

This mask is considered one of the most effective due to the fact that it promises to block at least 95% of the particles down to 0.3 microns in size. A phenomenon called Brownian motion details that when microscopic particles enter the N95 filter, they ping around like a ball in a pinball machine, increasing its chances of hitting the filter and impeding its movement.

https://smartairfilters.com/en/blog/diy-homemade-mask-protect-virus-coronavirus/

As mentioned previously, the Coronavirus is estimated to be smaller, and therefore it does not provide complete protection. The masks can be obtained in pharmacies, superstores, medical supply stores, and on the Internet. The World Health Organization has instructed health teams treating carriers or patients to respond hermetically, wearing a full protective suit.

Another concern is that the Coronavirus may also infect the lining of the eyes, which no mask promises to prevent. Surface contact can also cause infection. It is feared that the Coronavirus can live on surfaces for up to 9 days, so touching an infected surface with the Coronavirus, can cause infection. N99 masks are supposed to be the more effective of the two types of most popular masks, promising to block up to 99% of particles from penetrating its shield. However, these can be a bit difficult to breathe in. This mask may be unsuitable for children or people with breathing difficulties.

CLEANING PRODUCTS THAT DESTROY THE NOVEL CORONAVIRUS

SOAP AND WATER:

Just the friction from scrubbing with soap and water can break the Coronavirus protective envelope. Remember when you were a kid, and you played with sticky paint and glue. Remember how hard you had to scrub your hands from all directions rubbing and washing them well in order to remove the substance from your skin? You need to rub your hand for at least 60 seconds and then dry them with a disposable paper towel. If you are using a cloth towel, then leave it in a bowl of water with soap or one of the other disinfecting substances listed below for a while in order to destroy any virus particles that may have survived the initial handwashing.

BLEACH:

The Centers for Disease Control and Prevention recommends a diluted bleach solution (⅓ cup bleach per 1 gallon of water or 4 teaspoons bleach per 1 quart of water) for virus disinfection. Wear gloves while using bleach, and never mix it with anything except water (the only exception is when doing laundry with detergent). Do not keep the solution for longer than a few days because bleach will degrade in certain plastic containers.

Bleach can also corrode metal over time, so do not get into the habit of cleaning your faucets and stainless steel products with bleach. Bleach is harsh for many countertops as well. You should rinse surfaces with water after using bleach as a disinfecting agent to prevent discoloration or damage to the surface.

ISOPROPYL ALCOHOL:

Alcohol solutions with at least 70 % of alcohol are effective against the Coronavirus. Do not dilute the alcohol solution. Alcohol is generally safe for all surfaces but can discolor some plastics.

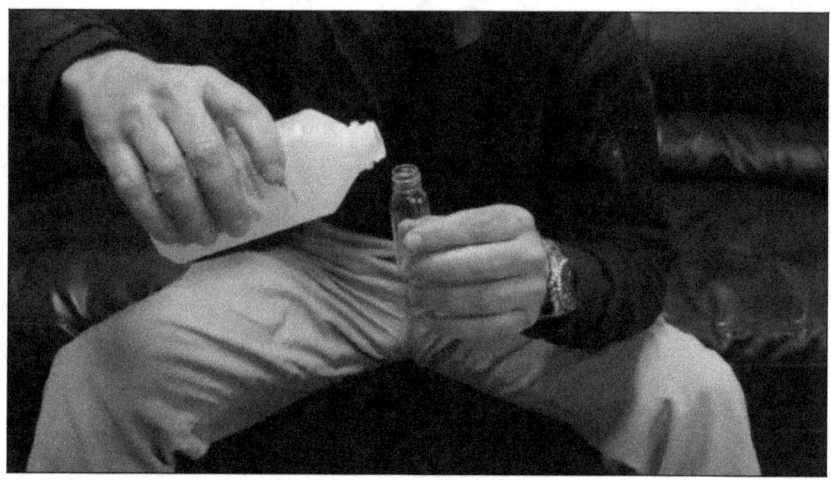

HYDROGEN PEROXIDE:

According to the CDC, household (3 percent) hydrogen peroxide is effective in deactivating rhinovirus (the virus that causes the common cold) within 6 to 8 minutes of exposure. Rhinovirus is more difficult to destroy than Coronaviruses, so hydrogen peroxide should be able to break down the Coronavirus in less time. Pour it undiluted into a spray bottle and spray it on the surface to be cleaned, but let it sit on the surface for several minutes. Hydrogen peroxide is not corrosive, so it's okay to use it on metal surfaces. But similar to bleach, it can discolor fabrics if you accidentally get in on your clothing.

Now we all witnessed people franticly storming stores to purchase disinfectants, alcohol-based gel, and other states of the art disinfection products.

What if you cannot buy these ready-made products, can you make your own?

Here is an example of a homemade, basic disinfecting solution that you can make: You need to get alcohol, not the consumable alcohol, it needs to be pure with at least 70% isopropyl. Though the CDC recommends 60%, I recommend a higher percentage because it seems the Coronavirus is so contagious. You want to be sure that you are completely terminating it.

Here's how to prepare the disinfectant:

Mix two-thirds of alcohol with 8-10 drops of natural oil. Mix everything thoroughly, and the staff is ready. Then you should put the solution into a spray bottle. I recommend you prepare several spray bottles. You can place one in your vehicle, one at your home, another at your workplace, in your gym bag, etc.

PROPER HANDWASHING:

A study published last year by the University of Glasgow found that hand washing in six stages is much more effective than regular 3-step hand washing that includes soaping/scrubbing, washing hands with water, and closing the tap.

And here's how the hand washing takes place in the six-step practice:

Preparation phase: Open the tap, wet your hands and apply soap

Step 1: Apply the soap from palm to palm.

Step 2: The right-hand scrubs the back of the left palm.

Step 3: Scrub finger to finger

Step 4: Be sure to wash the back of each palm.

Step 5: Wash thumbs thoroughly

Step 6: Hand-to-hand scrubbing and rotational movements.

Final Step: Dry your hands and wipe the tap.

The handwashing instructions also emphasize how to close the faucet, which may be contaminated. Therefore, its closure should be done using the elbow in places where there is a long handle for the faucet (as in hospitals and clinics), or by wiping it off with some disinfectant/soap and a paper towel just before throwing it into the trash can.

CHAPTER SEVEN

WHAT IF YOU HAVE A PET LIKE A DOG, CAT, ETC.?

If you own a pet like a dog or a cat, you are probably wondering what you should do to protect both yourself and them against the Coronavirus. The question may arise, "What if I get infected and become a carrier of the virus is it possible for me to give it to my pet?"

In Hong Kong: Dog found infected with Coronavirus - sent for isolation, fear of infection by animals.

Coronavirus first pet case: Hong Kong government announced that a dog was found to be infected with the Coronavirus. He has since been sent out for isolation; in the meantime, a new concern has emerged that the Novel Coronavirus can also spread through animals. It is estimated that the Coronavirus came to humans through bats carrying the virus, after being mutated by other Coronaviruses. So far, it has not been determined if there are any other new variation of animals that can carry the virus and infect humans. The exact details have not yet been disclosed as to the test circumstances the dog has undergone, but this is the first known case in which a dog contracted the Coronavirus. In the meantime, the pet has been placed in solitary confinement and is expected to undergo repeated tests to detect the virus. This case raises concerns that more animals have contributed to the rapid spread of the virus worldwide. In this case, isolation instruction may also be added for the animals found to be infected. Reported by CNBC

For example, there is a type of Coronavirus that infects chickens. Scientists in the state of Israel are working on a vaccine based on these strains of chicken Coronavirus. More on their work, further down this book.

What should you do if your dog or cat catches it?

Let's assume that you take your dog for a walk. Avoid letting your dog interact with other animals. Also, if you see other dogs don't touch or pet them. It is possible that the other dog's owner could be a carrier of the Coronavirus. What if he or she haven't developed any symptoms yet, however, they are contagious and just don't realize it yet. What if the other dog's owner sneezes or coughs on the dog and particles of saliva go all over the dog? If you pat the dog, you can get the virus on yourself and on your dog as well. In this case, if you are not living alone and you have other family members, then you put them at risk as well. As for the dog in Hong Kong, at the time of writing this book, they are still investigating this case. This is why it has not been confirmed definitively if dogs can get the virus.

CHAPTER EIGHT

HOW TO PREPARE AND STOCK UP FOR THE CORONAVIRUS PANDEMIC

Stocking up on pain and fever relievers, prescription drugs, electrolytes, and food are the most prudent ways to prepare for the novel Coronavirus pandemic. Preparation should not be that much different than preparing for emergencies like natural disasters such as earthquakes, floods, hurricanes and tornadoes, storms, etc.

It is very important not to panic and to prepare supplies and resources for a period of 10 to 16 weeks. You need to have a clean drinkable water supply for the estimated length of time. If you have a swimming pool, get special filters that can filter the water and give you clean drinking water just in case.

You should also stock food, the US Department of Homeland Security's emergencies and disaster prep site, https://www.ready.gov/pandemic, and check your regular prescription drugs to ensure a continuous supply is in your home. The site also recommends topping up on nonprescription drugs such as pain relievers, stomachache remedies, cough and cold medicines, fluids with electrolytes, and vitamins.

In addition, the US Center for Disease Control and Prevention (CDC) is encouraging people to identify household members who may be at greater risk of serious complications — such as the elderly or those with underlying health conditions. Pay particular attention in monitoring them for symptoms of the infection. General symptoms of the novel Coronavirus: fever, cough, runny nose, symptoms similar to those of the common cold or the flu.

The health agencies also recommend choosing a room in the home that can be used to separate household members should they become sick from those who are healthy, in order to stop the potential spread.

"Avoid sharing personal items like food and drinks. Provide your sick household members with clean disposable facemasks to wear at home, if available, to help prevent spreading COVID-19 to others. Clean the sick room and bathroom, as needed, to avoid unnecessary contact with the sick person," the CDC advises. In the meantime, health officials are continuing to urge people to stay at home if they are sick. Work from home if possible and keep up every day preventative actions.

This includes always covering coughs and sneezes with a tissue, washing hands frequently with soap and water for at least 20 seconds. Sanitize touchable surfaces and objects daily using regular household detergent and water. If soap and water are not available, hand sanitizer that contains 70% alcohol can be used. SEE ALSO

Here's how to tell if you have the Corona virus and when to see a doctor:

CHAPTER NINE

CORONAVIRUS TESTING – HOW TO TEST FOR CORONAVIRUS? DIFFERENT TYPES OF TESTS

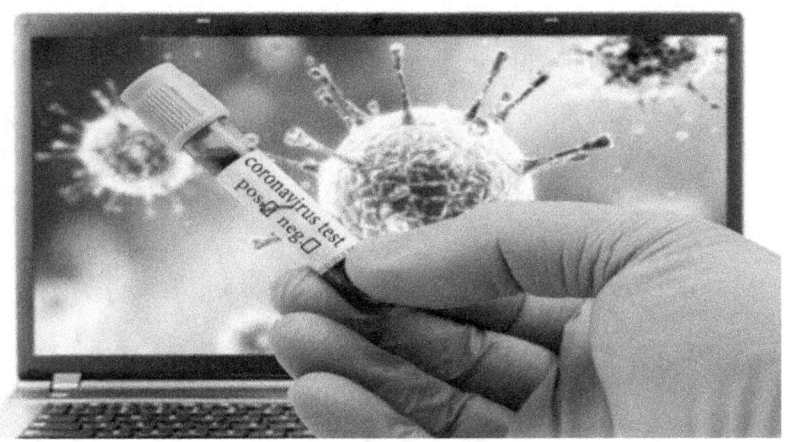

Patient screening and triage

Patients who present with fever and respiratory symptoms with an epidemiological link to COVID-19 should carry a high index of suspicion for the disease. The epidemiological link is defined as and may involve (a) travel to an area that experienced an outbreak, (b) close contact with an individual with confirmed or high risk of infection, or (c) close contact with an individual with respiratory symptoms who had been in a geographic location that witnessed an outbreak within 14 days prior to the onset of symptoms. As the geographic area of involvement is expanding, clinicians need to keep themselves updated about the list of affected countries and territories. Following several generations of spread with a country, local transmission of disease occurs, and patients may present with no history of travel to a location with a known outbreak.

Critically ill patients may present to the emergency department from the community or by inter-hospital transfer to the intensive care unit. In such instances, a detailed inquiry should be carried out to ensure appropriate screening and infection control precautions should be followed.

How to Get Tested for Coronavirus?

In case you feel your symptoms are specific to the Coronavirus, your healthcare provider can get in touch with CDC or the local healthcare departments for testing instructions. There are specific labs set up for conducting Coronavirus tests, so you may be directed to one of these labs.

There are different types of Coronavirus tests that can be done:

- Swab Test – In this case, a special swab is used to take a sample from your nose or throat

- Nasal aspirate – In this case, a saline solution will be injected into your nose, and then a sample is taken with a light suction

- Tracheal aspirate – In this case, a thin tube with a torch, also known as a bronchoscope, is put into your mouth to reach your lungs from where a sample is collected.

- Sputum Test – Sputum is thick mucus that gets accumulated in the lungs and comes out with a cough. During this test, you're required to cough up sputum in a special cup, or a swab is used to take a sample from your nose.

- Blood test – In this case, a blood sample is taken from a vein in the arm.

A rapid test has also been developed for the COVID-19, which involves taking samples from the nose, throat, and lungs. This ensures a speedy and accurate diagnosis and is used in all CDC-approved tests.

Before the test, the concerned health professionals may request you to wear a mask during the course of the test. In case there are any other steps that need to be taken, the healthcare professional can communicate that to you.

What are the risks associated while testing for the Corona virus?

During the test, you may feel a gagging sensation when the swab is inserted into your nose and throat. The nasal aspirate (withdrawn fluid) may especially seem a bit uncomfortable. However, all of these effects are temporary and will go away shortly after the test. In some cases of tracheal aspirate, there may be bleeding or infection. In the case of the blood test, no risks are observed. There may be slight swelling and pain in the area where the needle was inserted; however, it goes away pretty soon.

What next if a Coronavirus Test result is positive?

If your test results come out positive, then you may be affected by the Coronavirus. Although there are no specific treatments for the Coronavirus infection, the healthcare professional may suggest some steps that'll help you to relieve the symptoms.

Some of the steps you can follow to ease the symptoms are:

- Drinking a lot of fluids
- Getting plenty of rest
- Take over-the-counter medicines

In case your condition gets worse, or you show signs of pneumonia, you should get admitted to a hospital. Some of the common symptoms of pneumonia are severe cough, labored breathing, and high fever.

If you're diagnosed with Coronavirus, you should follow the below steps to prevent any spread of infection:

- Don't leave home, unless to get medical help
- Always wear a face mask in public places or when you're around other people
- Don't share any personal items such as drinking cups, eating plates, towels, or any other items with anybody.
- Always wash your hand thoroughly for at least 60 seconds. In case soap water is not available, you can use an alcohol-based sanitizer, which contains at least 70% alcohol.

Should your test results be negative, you can check with the healthcare professional whether any further tests are required. Then take precautions to prevent the infection.

On the other hand, it is better to avoid getting infected by the Coronavirus by following the below steps:

- Wash your hands thoroughly for at least 60 seconds and use alcohol-based sanitizers in the absence of soap-water
- Avoid touching your eyes, nose, or mouth a lot
- If possible, avoid being close to people who are sneezing or coughing
- Clean all household items which are frequently handled with a disinfectant spray

Can you get the Coronavirus a second or third time after you initially overcome it?

Not likely, like with common viruses, bacteria, and fungi, once someone had the sickness and he or she overcomes it, they have immunity to the intruder.

How did such a thing happen?

In most infections, something special happens in the body. The immune system "learns" the contaminant's structure and behavior and prepares for the possibility of a recurring infection. Cells called lymphocytes, which form in different parts of the lymphatic system, are responsible for this. Lymphocytes are divided into two subtypes - B cells that are responsible for antibody secretion and T cells that destroy infected cells. When a B cell encounters a foreign invader, it secretes an antibody that initiates an immune response and neutralizes the foreign invader. When a T cell encounters an alien invader, it attacks it and destroys it directly. The two work collaboratively, thanks to which the immune system is able to identify and act against any foreign invader.

This is actually the natural vaccination process of the body; it is in this way that vaccine injections work. Some diseases have an active vaccine, which contains parts of foreign bodies that cause the body to make antibodies on its own. The antibodies possess recall ability that remembers the foreign invader. It uses this memory capacity to identify and help the immune system to act quickly against recurrence. The passive vaccine, on the other hand, contains antibodies that are injected into the body and act against foreign invaders. So, you can say this type of antibody production is induced.

Much is still unknown about the Novel Coronavirus that has infected 6,194,533 people worldwide and with 376,320 deaths so far as of June 2- 2020, source World Health Organization. But as the United States and other countries confront the increasing threat of COVID-19, many have asked whether it's possible for patients to catch the Coronavirus more than once.

In mainland China, where the outbreak originated and where the majority of the cases occurred before widespread in Italy, there have been more than 100 reported cases of patients released from hospitals who later tested positive for the Coronavirus a second time, according to the Los Angeles Times. In at least one instance, a 36-year-old man died earlier this month in Wuhan, China, five days after health officials declared he had recovered and discharged him from the hospital. In

China's Guangdong province, health officials say 14 % of people who recovered in the province who were later retested were positive.

Similar cases have been reported in Japan and South Korea.

A woman working as a tour bus guide in Japan tested positive for Coronavirus for the second time after developing a sore throat and chest pain. She first tested positive in late January and was discharged from the hospital in early February after showing signs of recovery.

"Once you have the infection, it could remain dormant with minimal symptoms," Philip Tierno Jr., professor of microbiology and pathology at New York University, told Reuters last month. "And then you can get an exacerbation if it finds its way into the lungs," he said.

Scientists agree reinfection is an unlikely explanation for patients who test positive a second time, according to the Los Angeles Times. They note the possibility of testing errors, and the release of patients from hospitals too prematurely, as more than likely the reason for reports of patients who retest positive. "If you get an infection, your immune system is revved up against that virus," Keiji Fukuda, director of Hong Kong University's School of Public Health, told the Los Angeles Times. "To get reinfected when you're in that situation would be quite unusual unless your immune system was not functioning right," Fukuda told the papers that it's more likely patients are being released from hospitals while carrying dormant fragments of the disease that are not infectious but resemble the virus when tested. "The test may be positive, but the infection is not there," he said.In a hearing before the House Oversight and Reform Committee, Anthony Fauci, director of the National Institute of Allergy and Infectious Disease, was asked if people who have contracted the virus might now be immune. "We haven't formally proved it, but it is strongly likely that that's the case," Fauci said. "Because if this acts like any other virus, once you recover, you won't become re-infected."

Source: the Los Angeles times newspaper

CHAPTER TEN

CHILDREN CAN CONTRACT THE CORONAVIRUS LIKE ADULTS

A new study presents preliminary evidence that children can be infected with the Coronavirus just the same as adults. The findings also indicate that even if almost all children do not develop symptoms, this does not mean that they do not become infected, so they can be quiet carriers and infect more people. In December 2019, the Coronavirus first burst in the Hubei region of China. As soon as it became clear that there was an outbreak of a new human-infecting dangerous virus, which later became a pandemic, researchers began collecting data on the new disease, which mainly affects the respiratory system.

One of the characteristics identified was that while people over the age of 60 or with a history of background illnesses tend to develop more complications and mortality rates, children seem to experience a reversed condition where the morbidity rate is very low. However, child mortality was hardly observed. Among researchers' hypotheses that tried to explain the finding was the possibility that children are less likely to get infected with this virus or are infected but less susceptible to it. A preliminary study recently published in the MedXRIV database shows that children are probably less likely to develop significant symptoms but are less likely to contract the virus than adults.

Researchers from the Center for Disease Control and Prevention in Shenzhen, China, gathered information on 391 patients (187 men and 204 women) examined between January 14 and February 12 this year. They rated the severity of the disease in each patient according to 21 measures and symptoms, and additionally, they looked at metrics like age, gender, and closeness to other patients.

The researchers monitored and documented these patients for symptoms that confirmed exposure to the virus, infection duration, disease development, and recovery. They found that the average incubation time was about five days, and most patients developed symptoms within a maximum of two weeks. Patients aged 59-50 needed 32 days from the time of infection to recover, but the recovery time for young people was shorter: an average of 27 days at age 29-20. 1.3 percent of patients who participated in the study died of the disease.

Despite the above information, unfortunately, almost in every country, children and teens of various ages have died from Coronavirus complications. (Ages of 1, 5.10, 12, 16)

CHILDREN MAY BE CONTAGIOUS

To characterize the form of infection and the rate of infection, the researchers examined 1,286 people who had spent a long time with patients. They noticed that the infection rate dropped naturally as they made sure to isolate those who had symptoms of illness.

When analyzing the rate of infection by age, the researchers found that the severity of the disease on infected children was indeed lower than that of adults, as seen in other observations. However, the infection rate was similar for all the general population. Even if children do not develop symptoms, this does not mean that they will not become infected; they can become asymptomatic quiet carriers and infect more people.

This study has some limitations. Several teams collected the data, so there may be no uniformity in the working method and information. Therefore, there are some observed differences between the data. Also, the data on patients were collected from people who were already isolated, making it difficult to estimate the true infection rate in the general population. It has been observed that children who have been diagnosed with Novel Coronavirus are less asymptomatic than adults. Children are less susceptible to the virus than adults.

Finally, this study has not yet been peer-reviewed and has only been published in a research database. There may be further significant changes in the analysis of the results and conclusions of the researchers, according to comments from peer researchers.

CHAPTER ELEVEN

HOW TO GUIDE YOUR CHILD OR TODDLER TO AVOID CONTRACTING THE CORONAVIRUS

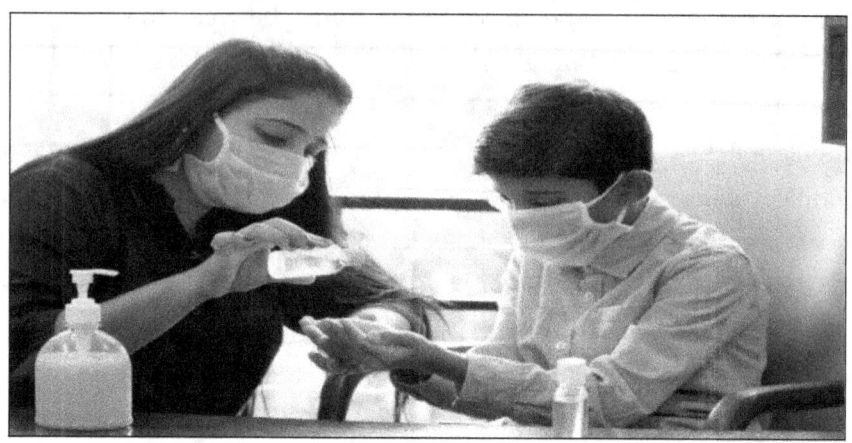

As a parent, not only do you need to make sure you don't catch the Coronavirus, you also have to educate your children on how not to get infected and to reduce their stress level as much as possible.

When children see their parents staying home and not going to work, they may see that as unusual and understand that something could be wrong. Children may also watch the news or may consequently end up seeing new reports on the status of the Coronavirus.

Parents may find it very challenging to explain the nature and dangers of what is currently happening because of the Coronavirus around the world.

First, you need to educate yourself about the virus and how to handle a world pandemic crisis. This can be done by educating you through reading, like you are presently doing, and obtaining information by watching videos like the ones included with this book.

This process could be an excellent tool for your child's education. Ideally, you want to ask your children what they already know or have heard or may have learned at school or through other sources about the Coronavirus.

You can also use your computer to show your children pictures and videos from the Internet on microscopic organisms such as viruses, fungi, and bacteria. This will help them understand and relate to the virus though it is invisible to the naked eye.

If you are fortunate enough and you to have a microscope at home, this is a great time to take it out and run some experiments with them.

Setting a good example and being creative

Children sometimes do not do what their parents tell them to do. This is why it's important to be an active role model, exhibiting smart and safe behavior by example through your actions.

For example, if you are washing your hands, have your children next to you. You could sing a song and have your children do the same while you are both washing your hands. You can also ask them questions that required them to think critically about why they are thinking the way they are about changes in their daily routine. For example, deconstruct the process of hand washing and have them explain to you why it is so exceedingly vital at this time.

You can also make your children responsible for all household safety by putting them in charge of safety enforcement protocols and reminding other family members about disinfecting and hygiene practices.

You can also use your children's toys to explain to them different principles like social distancing etc. You can take their toy cars or dolls and social distance them, in this way, your children can and will most likely learn through play.

Children also may feel that they are missing friends or relatives like grandma or grandpa or even uncle or auntie. The best way to explain why they can't visit them right now is by stressing the importance of limiting contact at this time. And then explain that older people are being affected more drastically than younger people at this time and it's just the best way to protect both relatives and friends for the time being.

As for children seven and above, you can use the instructional videos which are included with this book. As your children see you follow some of the protocols which are described in the book and videos, they will be more susceptible to the concepts and will understand better. For example, let's assume you are following my protocol on how to put gas in your car during this Coronavirus scary time. Give your smartphone to your child and ask them to film you as you follow the safety procedures described in this book. Not only will this activity be inclusive and fun, but it will also subliminally engage your child in a way that will help them to comprehend and understand these safety concepts more effectively. They see how to avoid becoming infected during these typical everyday activities; also, they witness the apparent danger and possibility of spreading the disease by not being mindful about the safety of others.

As you travel from place to place, practice these activities in various situations and environments. Your children's stress level will go down, and you can be more confident that you educated your child about the Coronavirus and how not to become infected.

Problems with testing

Multiple hospitals around the world are reporting a problem with testing when they test patients for the Coronavirus through the nose and throat and find the results are negative. Still, these results can be faulty since testing the same person's lungs high numbers of patients are found to have Coronavirus.

Why some people die from the Coronavirus complication and some are not

While there is a very complex medical explanation, I will try to explain it to you in the simplest manner. A good, normally functioning immune system is like a person who is close to dehydration and then receives a cup of water with a straw compared to an immune system that is overreacting and giving that same person a blast of water from a fire hose.

I hope you understand now that in cases of Coronavirus complications and mortality in most cases is because of the immune system overreacting and eventually killing the body.

Please view the following videos for an explanation of the whole process in a visual manner:

https://youtu.be/5DGwOJXSxqg
https://youtu.be/I-Yd-_XIWJg

CHAPTER TWELVE

SAFETY PROTOCOLS

RUNNING/WALKING:

It's interesting to note that the Coronavirus can stay in the air for up to three hours after someone has coughed or sneezed. This is troublesome given that you could potentially catch the virus hours after another runner, infected with the virus, has used your running path.

Follow the below protocol as suggested: Try to change your running routine. For example, where I live, I often run around a lake, but there are also many others that are doing the same. This is why I regularly change my running routine. I either choose a place where people usually don't run, or I run on a treadmill inside my home.

Running on a treadmill is by far the safest way to run or walk nowadays. Now, if you still want to run outside, consider wearing a mask. However, I want to remind you that running with a mask can be cumbersome, and it also will not provide sufficient protection against the Coronavirus since it's not proven to be impervious to penetration by its small size, as I described in the book previously.

CONVENIENCE STORES

The safety protocols I'm recommending here have two perspectives: First, from the perspective of a store employee and second from a buyer or shopper.

Store employees: Store employees face multiple risks, not just when they are behind the counter, but when doing other work-related tasks. Some of these tasks include stocking shelves, freezers, refrigerators, snack bar, coffee machines, maintaining inventory, office, and front desk or restroom areas. In everything that they do, they are interacting with potentially infected merchandise, instruments, tools, and building structures. The most important thing is to not become ill in the first place. Employees that are not feeling well should definitely consider not going to work.

In this protocol, you'll need first to wear a mask, and then put a line of colored reflective tape on the floor roughly 2m (6 ft) away from the cash register. Ask the shoppers that approach the counter not to cross the line and to wait there until you call them. Ask them to place the merchandise on the store counter, while you step to the side. Then ask the buyer to step back behind the line while you scan the merchandise, then put the merchandise in a bag and ask the buyer to pay for his or her purchase. It is also good to wear surgical gloves and to avoid touching your face or head. If you don't want, or cannot wear gloves, then have a disinfecting gel or alcohol spray that you can spray on your hands and on the spray bottle. You'll want to use it frequently, especially when you take your lunch break, bathroom break, office break, or for a cigarette break.

As a buyer/shopper: As described earlier in this book in a gas station scenario, you may need to go inside the store either to pay for the gas or to purchase something else. It's important to prepare before entering the store by disinfecting yourself with alcohol gel or an alcohol spray. You can also wear gloves, but you'll also need to spray the gloves with alcohol spray before you enter the store. Always think about other people that you may have interactions with and be mindful of their safety as well as your own. You'll need to carry a Ziploc or plastic bag in order to give the cashier your cash and then accept the change. If you are using a credit/debit card, place it inside the Ziploc bag after using it. If you bought additional items, ask the cashier to put them in a plastic or paper bag for you. Then when you get to your destination, use the alcohol spray to spray the contents of the bag to disinfect its contents.

If you purchase coffee or another drink that you intend to drink immediately, it is important to disinfect the bottle or the drink container. If the coffee has a plastic lid, make sure to disinfect it as well before you put the drink to your mouth. Remember, the Coronavirus can stay on surfaces for up to nine days. This is the reason why it's so important to practice these laborious procedures. Practicing these procedures is not only vital to avoid catching or spreading the virus but, most importantly, to ensure we can put an end to the catch and spread cycle all around the world. Please do your part as a decent human being, be safe, and act responsibly!

RESTAURANT OR PUB

In this situation, the recommended protocol is for the establishment's guests, waitresses, hosts, busboys, bouncers, etc.

During infectious disease situations, more specifically, the Coronavirus, it's a good idea to carry a disinfectant spray bottle with you. When you sit at the table, spray the menu with the alcohol/disinfectant spray. If the menu is made from paper, you may not be able to spray it with the alcohol. Therefore, it's a good idea to carry some rubber gloves with you as well. Once you're finished looking at the menu, and you're ready to order give the menu back to the waitress.

The waiters will bring you your drinks if it's a cold drink in a glass or cup spray both the glass and the cup and including the lip of the glass or cup. For example, if you order an orange juice, ice water, or a coke, ask for a sealed straw and then use it. If you order a beer in a bottle or in a beer mug, disinfect the bottle and the lip as mentioned in the previous paragraph. For utensils (forks, knives, spoons, etc.) make sure to disinfect them as well with an alcohol spray before use. When you receive the check, and you pay with cash or with a debit or credit card.

If you pay cash and you are supposed to get change, use a Ziploc/plastic bag to store the change. If you need to sign the check, then try to use your own pen, if you have to use the establishment's pen disinfect it before usage. As for your debit or credit card, since other people may have to touch it, it may become infected, put it in the Ziploc/plastic bag and disinfect it later. Before you get into your vehicle or touch your keys, it is important to disinfect your hands with the alcohol spray or disinfecting wipes to avoid contaminating them.

If you are a waiter, hostess, staff, etc. it's important to make sure that you are not sick. Also, it's important to wash your hands with soap and water frequently to discourage infection, contamination, and to maintain a high level of personal hygiene. The establishment may require you to wear a mask, please remember that the mask does not protect you 100%, as you interact with the guests, it's important to try and maintain as much distance as possible, ideally 6-7 feet when possible.

Since the Coronavirus is an airborne virus, it may help if you are able to hold your breath while serving the food or drinks. Remember, the less time you spend next to the table, the more you reduce the likelihood of getting sick. Also, when applicable, ask your guests to cough or sneeze into their elbow or into a napkin.

As for bouncers, your job is a little bit trickier since you may have to deal with intoxicated/unruly people or guests that may be throwing up, sneezing, coughing, or misbehaving. I recommend using a body temperature thermometer that every guest will have to undergo at the time of admission to the premises. If they have a fever, they should not be allowed access to the premises. The establishment may also require you to wear a mask. In this case, remember the mask does not provide you sufficient protection, and this is why it's important to stop your breathing if someone is sneezing or coughing at or near you. Lastly, it's important not to touch the face or the head and to wear rubber gloves.

As the establishment's cashier all the cash money and the receipts need to be disinfected, make sure that all the people involved in this process have disinfected or washed their hands with soap and water before and after the process.

BANK & POST OFFICE

The safety protocol that I recommend using in a bank/post office setting is divided into four scenarios:
1. ATM outside the bank/ ATM machine in the bank/Post office sending mail/package drop off
2. Drive-through service
3. A teller inside the bank/post office
4. A loan officer

1. ATM machine inside/outside the bank or Post office mail/package drop off:

First, it's important to make sure that you are not sick and that you are constantly disinfecting yourself and your hands responsibly! You may also consider using rubber/plastic gloves. When you open the bank/post office front door, make sure you are using gloves. If you don't have gloves, make sure you are carrying an alcohol spray bottle to spray the door handle or alcohol gel to clean your hands. Be aware of your body, especially your hands. Don't touch your face or your head. It is a good idea to have the ATM card already in your pocket or inside a Ziploc bag along with something to clean the ATM dial keys if you don't have gloves. Consider the keypad or the monitor to be contagious. Consider any packaging or label materials potentially contaminated as well.

If you don't have gloves and you are unsure when you will be able to wash your hands, try to be certain about the mailing transaction you want to conduct to minimize time duration and unnecessary exposure. Disinfect the ATM buttons by spraying some disinfectant or alcohol spray on a piece of napkin and gently wipe the ATM buttons before you insert your ATM card into the machine slot. If you use your finger to make the selection, be sure not to touch your face or any part of your clothes with that finger.

If you make a withdrawal, take the money, and put it inside the Ziploc bag, remember the money may be contaminated. Disinfect your returned ATM card before returning it to your purse/wallet. Otherwise, place it in a Ziplock/plastic bag.

When returning to your car, use the alcohol gel or spray and disinfect yourself. If you used gloves, make sure to take off the gloves before getting into your car. The proper way to remove gloves is to first spray them with the alcohol spray, and only after you have sprayed them can you remove them.

2. **Drive-through service:** I recommend making sure to wear gloves or disinfectant or alcohol spray your hands when you receive the plastic withdrawal/deposit container. Use your own pen to fill in the withdrawal or deposit slip. When you receive the container back, with cash, card, receipt, or mailing package, put them inside a Ziploc/plastic bag and then disinfect and sterilize your hands.

3. **Dealing with a teller inside the bank:** Usually, when you need to see the bank teller, you first need to fill out a transaction form/s. Try to think ahead and take a pen or plastic gloves with you. Avoid using the bank's pen, if possible. You should consider wearing a mask when you are waiting in line. Make sure to face away or at an angle from the people that are in front and behind you. When it's your turn, do not lay your elbows or arms on the counter. Provide that bank teller with the signed form, deposit, or receive money. Put it in a Ziploc/plastic bag, like before. After leaving the bank, disinfect and sterilize yourself with the alcohol spray or gel.

4. **Dealing with a loan officer:** To see the loan officer, you may need to sign a list and most likely be asked to sit down and wait for your turn. When you sit down, it's important not to touch the seat or armrest with your hands. If there are magazines or anything else lying in front of you, don't touch them. You should consider wearing a mask, rubber gloves and have your own pen. Also, consider possessing an alcohol spray bottle or sanitizer gel so that you can sterilize yourself. You may also consider asking the bank loan officer to disinfect their hands as well before conducting any transactions. You can state that you are only requesting this as another layer of safety for the sake of both of you.

SENDING OR - RECEIVING AMAZON OR EBAY PACKAGES AND MAIL:

Since the Coronavirus can stay on surfaces for up to nine days, it is very plausible that you can get the Coronavirus through contact with mail. Therefore, the safety protocols recommended are divided into three categories:
1. The delivery driver
2. Packages left at your doorway
3. Mail-in your mailbox

1. As the driver and delivery person, it's a good idea for you to wear a mask as well as gloves. Remember that the Coronavirus can stay in the air for up to three hours. So as a precaution, it is a good idea to hold your breath as you deliver the package. If you need the customer to sign for the package, hold the writing pad, and ask them to sign, they might use their own pen or your pen. If they are using your pen, make sure to disinfect it with alcohol spray before and after use. Also, if you ring the doorbell or buzzer, make sure to sanitize your finger. You can also use a specially assigned pen or object expressly for pressing doorbells.

2. If the package is left at your doorway: In this situation, you may want to consider that the deliveryman/woman may have coughed or sneezed outside your doorway. Coronavirus can stay up to three hours in the air if there is no wind. It is possible that when you are retrieving your package, you may breathe in the virus. This is why it's important to take precautions. Wear a mask, though the mask may not provide you with 100% protection. Partial protection is better than none at all. Remember, it's important to have a good immune system in order to fight off the virus, and to potentially minimize the likelihood of contracting other viruses, bacteria, or fungi.

If a delivery man rings your doorbell and hands you a package, it's important to use your own pen if you need to sign. Wear a mask, and if you can, try to hold your breath as you are taking the package and completing the transaction as soon as possible. Dispose of the wrapper or box your package was delivered in as soon as you are done. Remember to disinfect the door handle from both sides, then the doorbell button, next to the package, and lastly, your hands.

3. Mail-in your mailbox: You may find letters, discount vouchers, magazines, etc. in your house or apartment mailbox. In this scenario, I recommend using gloves before getting your mail, put the mail into a nylon bag, and then disinfect the mail content with an alcohol spray. Spray each mail component at least two times in five-minute intervals; only then should you open the mail

YOUR CELL PHONE, IPAD OR TABLET PC:

One of the most contaminated tools we are always using and have with us is our cell phones. Today's smartphones are used far more than any other computer device. During the Coronavirus pandemic or any other infectious disease scenario, we need to bear in mind that each time we touch or hold our phone, we are potentially infecting it with a contagious virus. Therefore, we always have to bear in mind that if we intend to use our phone to make a call or to check emails, interact with social media, watch YouTube videos, etc. we should disinfect and sterilize it with alcohol spray. It's also important to disinfect the phone case as well.

How to disinfect your phone?

First, sterilize your hand with an alcohol gel, spray, or with soap and water.

Second, spray the phone from both sides from the back and then from the sides, where the buttons are located. Pay attention that some older phones may be sensitive to moisture, so you may need to wipe your phone with alcohol wipes instead.

In any case, remember not to use your hands or fingers to touch your head or face. This practice will decrease the chances of you contracting the virus. This protocol is applied not just for cell phones, but also for any other electronic device such as iPads, tablets, PCs, Bluetooth devices and regular earphones, smart watches, etc.

THE SEAT – AS A PASSENGER IN A TUBULAR VEHICLE SUCH AS A BUS, TRAIN AND ON BOARD AN AIRPLANE.

The recommended protocol for this type of transportation scenario is very important because, in this set-up, you're most likely going to encounter many other people that may unknowingly be carriers of the Coronavirus or other infectious diseases that could compromise your immune system. I recommend wearing a face mask, in some cases, even a mask/headgear that can cover your whole head. However, bear in mind that we are approaching warmer weather around April, May, and the summer months. If the virus is still in play, it will make it very hard to function with a mask/headgear, especially in hot and humid weather.

It's important to carry with you on buses, trains and subways plastic gloves, hand sanitizer, alcohol/disinfectant wipes, and or spray with some paper towels or napkins and a large Ziploc bag. On a commercial flight, you may have issues with the alcohol spray. Consider an appropriate bleach mixture spray in small enough bottles that the TSA will allow you to carry it on board the airplane. Also, a good alternative is hand sanitizer. Research or contact your airline to determine which is permitted.

When you're about to get take your seat, first, wipe the seat, its immediate surroundings, headrest, armrest, food tray, window, and the back of the seat in front of you. As you are seated, keep in mind that the passenger before you may have sneezed or coughed on the surrounding surfaces and floor. Therefore, you have to assume that the bottoms of your shoes are contaminated. When you get home or to your work, spray the bottoms of your shoes with the alcohol/disinfectant before entering the room and removing your shoes.

When on buses, trains, and airplanes, it's always better to sit next to the window for the following reasons. You can turn your face away from everybody else. You can avoid coming into contact with people, especially sick people that are moving down the aisle. If the passenger(s) sitting next to you sneezes or coughs, you have your own escape corner.

On a commercial flight, many people are concerned about the air circulating. You should be aware that the air circulating on a commercial flight goes through so many filters that it's almost identical to a surgery room, so the chance of contracting the virus is "almost" 0. You can use the air coming from the vent above you to blow the air away from you. In this way, you push away the inhaled/exhaled breath of other passengers that are sitting next to you.

When you are waiting in the terminal, you need to follow the applicable protocols, as previously stated in this book, when buying food, drinks, magazines, books, and other items. While you are waiting to get on your flight, stand away from the line, observe and, at the appropriate time, advance, rush into the line and board the plane.

The purpose of possessing a Ziploc/plastic bag, in all the various scenarios, is to act as a container carry all napkins, wipes, cleaning, and disinfecting material that you are traveling with. If you buy the Ziploc/plastic bags in large packages, you can just discard each into a trash can once you're out of the transportation terminal.

PUBLIC RESTROOMS AND WATER FOUNTAINS:

In different day-to-day scenarios, you may find yourself using the restroom or a water fountain in educational institutes, malls, stores, fast food establishments, parks, sports facilities, etc.

Water fountains can be highly contagious. If you have alcohol/sanitizing spray, you should disinfect the actuator button. It's essential to first let the water run for a few seconds and then drink. Remember, after you drink, do not wipe your lips with your hands or shirtsleeve. Instead, use hand sanitizer/alcohol to clean your hands because the user before you may have been contagious.

In regard to public restrooms: They can vary from being extremely clean and sanitized to extremely dirty and contagious. Let's assume that you are driving, and you feel an urge to go to the restroom. If you can, choose a restroom in an establishment that you have good experiences with. In many cases, it's good to have and wear gloves. In this way, you can best protect yourself when you open doors and handle the restroom door keys. Once in the restroom, lock the door, prep the toilet seat, do your business, flush, and dispose of the gloves. Wash your hands, put on another pair of gloves, return the key, and leave the establishment without much concern of contaminating yourself or others.

In case you don't have gloves or hand sanitizer and you have touched the establishment's door with your bare hand/s, you have to assume that your hands are now infected with the virus or an infectious disease. As you get into the restroom, wash your hands with soap and water, roll some toilet paper on your clean hand, do your business, and before you leave, wash your hands again with soap and water for at least 60 seconds.

When it comes to drying your hands, I do not recommend using bathroom air blowers as recent studies show that they are infested with bad stuff. Use paper towels instead. Take at least two paper towels. Dry your hands with one paper towel, then discard it and use the other to open the restroom door. Be sure only to use it on one side to prevent your hand from coming into contact with the doorknob.

FAST FOOD

Because of our very busy modern lifestyles, many people eat at fast food establishments in the United States. It could be McDonald's, Wendy's, Burger King, Taco Bell, or anyone of many other fast-food franchises. You can drive-through in your vehicle, order through a microphone and speaker system, pay from your vehicle, and get your food from a service window. In some countries, the fast-food can be from a falafel stand or any other street vehicle or cart set up.

In both cases, employees are instructed to keep a high standard of sanitation. However, because of the nature of the Coronavirus and other viruses, someone could be a carrier of the virus and not show any obvious sign. Since most of these employees are usually using gloves and practice well-crafted food handling safety procedures such as wearing hairnets/covers to prevent hair falling into prepared food, frequently washing their hands, continually changing gloves, avoiding sneezing or coughing into their gloves, etc. they are less likely to transfer the virus into the food they prepare.

However, if the cashier at the drive-through window does not have gloves, doesn't constantly clean their hands with alcohol/disinfecting spray or gel, or is unaware of infectious disease safety protocols, you may still be able to become infected. The drive-through attendant may potentially have come into contact with a sick or infected person unknowingly when giving the customer food and/or exchanging payment and change. They can then unknowingly give the virus to other customers, continuing the cycle and spreading it throughout the community.

To prevent this potential weak link in the fast-food industry, it's up to you to ensure that before you serve or touch your food, ensure that you follow responsible sanitation and hygiene practices. When handling money as well as your debit or credit card exchange, the protocol I recommend is for drive-through window attendants to ensure they are following smart, safe food and currency handling procedures by constantly cleaning hands and wearing gloves. Avoid breathing in other's direct breath when interacting in the drive-through and do not sneeze on people or their food. Customers should do the same with the addition of putting received change or cards inside a Ziploc/plastic bag and disinfecting them at home with alcohol spray, especially before replacing them back into your wallet or purse.

As for drinks and fries that you may get with your order, make sure to disinfect the drink cup, and the fry container. If you are still paranoid about the chances of contamination or the server using unprotected hands while spreading the salt on your French fries, you can take the extra safety step of asking them not to put any salt on your fries. You can always carry a salt jar or packets in your vehicle to use.

AS A POLICE OFFICER OR SECURITY OFFICER

Besides worldwide medical teams facing the Coronavirus and putting themselves at great risks, other public safety services, and first responders such as police officers and security personnel need to take precautions as well. The safety protocols that I developed for police officers are my recommendations and should not replace your current department protocols; instead, please examine my suggestions. If they fit and make sense, you are most welcome to use and adopt them.

As a police officer, traffic stops are one of the most dangerous tasks you have to perform. Any vehicle that you may stop for a regular speeding or traffic violation could end up with a gunfight or assault on you, the officer. To make things worse, the Coronavirus is an invisible enemy that can put you, your family, and your co-workers all in great danger.

The safety protocols that I am suggesting are intended to minimize your exposure to the virus. Let's assume you see a vehicle not obeying a stop sign. You stop the vehicle by getting behind him/her, turn your unit red lights and sirens on and command him/her to stop the vehicle.

At this point, you then approach the driver, asking the driver to lower his/her window and give you their driver's license and registration. At this point, you are putting yourself in great danger of contamination. The driver could be infected, or a no sign carrier of the Coronavirus or even an ailing patient.

In this situation, you the officer can remotely instruct the driver, that for everyone's safety and because of the current infectious disease pandemic you need him/her to put his/her driving license and registration underneath the left windshield wiper of their vehicle and then to get back into the vehicle and to put his/her hands on the steering wheel.

To minimize risks to the vehicle driver and passengers, make sure to sanitize your hands and gloves before any encounter with each vehicle you stop.

When you walk toward the stopped vehicle, take the driving license and registration form under the left windshield wiper. You can examine and monitor the driver and potential passengers through the window. Then take it to your unit, check on your unit's computer, and validate the information. After that, you should write the ticket or warning and then put it underneath the left windshield wiper.

What if window tinted black or dark?

There may be situations that you, the officer, may have to speak to the people in the vehicle. At any given minute, you can instruct the vehicle occupants to get out of the car and try to maintain proximity of 6 to 7 feet distance from them. This protocol is not one that solves all police officers' challenges since many times as a police officer, you have to pat down or search the person of the suspect. This is why carrying and using the N 95 mask along with gloves, and disinfectant/alcohol spray should be considered.

What does the Officer do if they have to arrest? Should the Officer have extra masks and gloves for the suspects when transporting them in a police vehicle? The Officer should always carry additional protective equipment to use in such situations when needed.

As security personnel, sometimes you could be scheduled to work 24 hours a day, day and night. Checking doors and gates to be sure they are locked, inspecting fences, patrolling on foot, on a bicycle or in a vehicle. You may come into contact with many people, make sure to wear gloves, don't touch your face or head, and always carry hand sanitizer as well as an alcohol spray. You may wonder why I am not saying that you must wear a protective mask; it's well-known now that the mask does not protect you against the coronavirus; it is only a prevention tool for people that might be already sick. That is being said, and I believe this, it's important to wear a protective mask because of other sicknesses and diseases that a protective mask may protect you from. Furthermore in this matter, police units/vehicles need to be modified inside in of the vehicle, in order to create a safe environment for the officers sitting in the front of the vehicle as well as for the suspects that might sit in the same vehicle.

ECONOMIC CRISIS RECOVERY BOOK SECTION

CHAPTER 13

YOU LOSE YOUR JOB DUE TO THE CORONAVIRUS PANDEMIC WHAT SHOULD YOU DO FROM HERE?

The Novel Coronavirus world pandemic has caused a major economic crisis, one that will ring in the halls of human history for a very long time. Many people, who held a stable job, may now find that after the world crisis is over, their circumstances have changed dramatically as the result of many companies and businesses closing and not being able to generate income for weeks or months resulting in employee layoffs. These employees leave, some with little financial compensation, some without any pay either furloughed or fired. What should you consider doing if you are one of those individuals? Losing your job under such dire circumstances may be a very shocking experience for you. It could put a lot of pressure on a person and add high tension to your relations with your spouse or family.

It is very important to get back on your feet as soon as you can. Try to look at this as an opportunity instead of a punishment. Maybe it's time for you to reassess your skill set, your passions for other areas of employment, and see if is the time for a career change or find a job at another company.

Your first line of temporary income will be your State Unemployment funds; if you meet the criteria, you may be able to claim its benefit. It's important to know that in many cases, the unemployment benefit is not enough and should be considered only as a temporary source of income that is meant to support you for a specific period of time while you are looking for new employment.

During this layoff period, it's important also to update your resume and make sure that your resume has several versions, each version should be tailored according to different job types. For example, a friend of mine lost his job after working for 20 years as a personal trainer in one of the casino hotels in Las Vegas. He met with me and asked me what he should do. I sat down with him and showed him how to create two different versions of his resume one resume for a personal trainer position and the second for a security job.

In addition to the two jobs he has held a few years back, he attended my school of Krav Haganah [defensive tactics] instructor program. I suggested that he could use this ability to not only enroll private students and provide private defensive tactics training. To this suggestion, he also added a fitness center supplementing his defensive tactics/self-defense class. Furthermore, because he had his qualifications on hand in the form of his resume, I was able to connect him with a friend of mine that was about to launch a new fitness business in Las Vegas.

I hope that from this example, you see why it's good to have various skills and certifications. The more certifications and skills you have, the more options you're going to have. I know no one solution can fit all scenarios. It's different if you are in your early 20s verse if you are in your 40s or 50s, and you faced with losing your job. I'm asking you to consider understanding that the Coronavirus crisis has just expedited the progression of global changes.

That on the way to happening in the next 5 to 10 years as artificial intelligence and robots are being chosen to replace many human jobs. This is why you should consider looking at your situation as an excellent opportunity to do a career change, to shift the tides, and alter your potential course for the better.

My advice to you is to go to a quiet place where you can focus and prioritize your thoughts and write down how you would like your life to look in the next 3 to 5 years from now. Look back at your life 3 to 5 years, if you don't like where you are now then your next 3 to 5 years could be exactly the same unless you make a drastic change and some smart adjustments. When I consult people, I always encourage them to try to pursue their passions when they choose a career as much as possible. This is especially possible if you take the time to evaluate what is important to you and use this knowledge to align yourself with a job that not only provides financial gain but makes your life feel fulfilling and meaningful. You may also consider going back to school, college, or university. If you are approved for a grant, financial aid or student loans in the US, you're going to be able to advance your education and your life as well as potentially be able to use some of the funds for financial support.

Again, in the US, many veterans don't know that they can use their VA benefits in a trade school or vocational school, similar to the way colleges and universities function. Veterans may be entitled to their vocational rehabilitation fund and others that veterans and their family members are entitled. In the United States, there are various states that provide funds for training certifications that can lead to a job. In the state of Nevada, for example, it's called the "workforce." I know this book will also be bought outside of the United States. Please don't be discouraged. Many other countries have similar, if not sometimes even better similar funding structures that support career and job opportunities.

As I mentioned before, robots and artificial intelligence are going to take many jobs and replace much of the workforce as we currently have. This is why there are many job opportunities and careers that you can do online. The fastest way to earn certifications is through Udemy; it is an online training platform that one can obtain his or her certification through various certification programs that are prepared by many professionals. A friend of mine was interested in getting into the cybersecurity field, I guided him to Udemy, and after three months he got multiple cybersecurity certifications that opened many new lucrative doors for him.

Now, if you are an entrepreneur, and have great communication skills, enjoy working alone as well as with a team, the one lucrative career that I identified to be the most powerful and rewarding is the joint venture broker certification program that my friend, Sohail Khan, is running.

Here is some detailed description of his program and how one could potentially create many lucrative opportunities for yourself and your loved ones. Just to give you an idea, the bare minimum that one needs to be a successful joint venture broker is a smartphone. Of course, you could use Other electronics, offices, etc. but it's not necessary. For example, you could broker a deal or an opportunity between two or more companies. You can potentially make hundreds of thousands, if not millions of dollars, as a partner or as a broker.

CHAPTER 14

ONE OF THE MOST POWERFUL & LUCRATIVE PROFESSION: JOINT VENTURE BROKERING

The role of joint venture broker changes depending upon the nature of the joint venture. The joint venture broker might be a person who finds joint venture partners or the person who sets up the deal. In both cases, the joint venture broker is compensated for his or her role by taking a percentage of the profits. Joint venture brokering is not a difficult concept to understand. Just imagine an orchestra. Surely, such an ensemble wouldn't be able to play marvelous music without the conductor? The conductor simply brings all the band members together and instructs them on how to proceed with a masterpiece. The conductor doesn't have to play any musical instruments; he just needs a good working knowledge of music. The scope of joint ventures can be arranged within the limits of your imagination. A car dealer can offer a free dinner at a local restaurant to anyone who comes in for a test drive—resulting in both the restaurant and the car dealer getting more customers to come and potentially add to their customer list. A sporting goods store can form a relationship with a health club or gym, each sending the other customers for fitness and equipment purchases. An electricity company agrees to include an ad for an appliance dealer in its next billing letter, reaching every utility user in the region. The electricity company is happy because they reduce their cost of mailing as a result of the appliance dealer paying a small fee for each insert. The appliance dealer is satisfied because they piggy-back on the electricity company's material, gaining access to all their customers, with less cost than if they were to conduct a mailing campaign of their own from scratch.

Joint venture brokering appeals to many entrepreneurs because it offers a way to earn really good money without having to create your own product, set up and implement any marketing strategies (although for some types of joint ventures, a knowledge of marketing is essential) and, more often than not, without having to invest anything financially. The joint venture broker essentially determines the type/s of resources a client needs, aligns, and mediates a symbiotic collaborative deal with other respective clients to determine what can be offered to joint venture partners who have those resources. The joint venture broker then works out how to present the offer to joint venture partners so that they see the offer as a "win-win-win" situation. (The three "wins" are a win for the client, a win for the joint venture partner, and a win for the customer as well.)

Approaching potential joint venture partners in the right way is vital to the outcome of the joint venture. The joint venture broker's role is to assist the client in convincing other potential partners who have never heard of that client to enter a joint venture deal through a well-crafted joint venture proposal. In most instances, the joint venture broker has already determined what a potential joint venture partner can gain from the deal. Having done the appropriate research, they know who needs what resources and how to find others to provide those resources.

Your choice of share/fee set up would, and should, depend on a careful study of the joint venture. If you are certain that the joint venture will meet your expectations, then a percentage system would be the best option (and most profitable for *you*) to take. If you have doubts as to whether or not the joint venture would/could achieve "blockbuster status," then a fixed rate may be the best route to take. Of course, you'll need to be more than just a joint venture broker to justify a share equal to that of each of the partners; you'll have to commit much labor toward the joint venture. Once you have decided on a payment scheme, you have to inform the partners of it at the earliest possible time. This will avoid the possibility of being undercut; that is, being neglected after they have taken over the joint venture.

To better protect your interests, put your chosen payment scheme in writing, and have the partners attest to it verifying that they have read and agree to the terms you have given. Bear in mind if you must discover the joint venture partners and to educate them on the subject of joint ventures, as the broker, you can construct a sales letter for the deal. Look over everything to make sure it all goes smoothly, manage the whole deal, etc. You may be able to get a much higher percentage (like 40% or so). Joint venture brokering is such a lucrative and exclusive field. Knowing all the advantages that you can derive from a career as a joint venture broker will develop a love for this job within you as I have. Loving your work, of course, is essential to your success.

Joint Venture Brokering is a highly creative business. It may not seem apparent right now but, trust me, there is more creativity involved in joint venture brokering than in any other field of marketing. Joint venture brokering, being the highly creative avenue that it is, will require a passion for the business. This is why you should love what you're doing. When you're passionate about your career, it will feel less like work and more like fun. It will also spark your creative genius, consequently leading to more success in your deals.

Let's take a look at the benefits that can be brought about from being a joint venture broker:

1. You don't need to spend years building your customer list and constantly trying to develop a better relationship with your subscriber base.
2. You don't need to keep track of the sales made, of how much money is owed to whom, of fulfilling the product and sending it out, etc.
3. You just step in, leverage those resources, and make colossal profits by bringing people together and contributing to others.
4. You will be known as an expert that makes things happen, and more opportunities will fall into your lap.
5. There will always be a need for a joint venture broker as long as businesses are seeking fresh ideas to expand their enterprises, increase their profits, and seeking other businesses that complement theirs.
6. As a joint venture broker, your market is not seasonal in nature. Demand for your services run for the whole duration of each and every passing year.

Not only is joint venture brokering a great way of earning a fantastic living (potentially 6 or even 7 figures a year), it is also a marvelous way of positioning yourself as an established authority in the marketing field.

To be a successful joint venture broker, a person MUST possess the following skills:

1. A good knowledge of your industry.
2. A comprehensive and diverse network of contacts.
3. Excellent communication and negotiating skills.
4. A creative mindset.
5. A will to succeed.

There is no better time than right now (especially when businesses are looking to engage in more partnerships to survive) to become a JV Broker. You will not only help companies or even your own clients to

If this opportunity interests, you Sohail Khan's 'Certified JV Broker' Boot camp programs are the perfect opportunity to get into brokering joint ventures!

More details on Sohail Khan's Boot camp and Home Study Programs here: www.BrokeringBootcamp.com

CHAPTER 15

WORKING FROM HOME

Necessary social distancing guidelines and attempts to prevent large numbers of infections among employees and coworkers during the Coronavirus global pandemic are forcing hundreds of millions of people all around the world to start to work from home. If you are one of those people who are suddenly forced to work from home, the process could be challenging. This is why I decided to include a chapter that will help you deal with working from home. The term working from home is not just about working from your apartment or house. It can also include working from a hotel room that you may have been confined to or any other set up that is outside of the regular workplace that you go to every day and return from.

The information I will share with you in this chapter is based on my personal experience. When I started my own business 20 years ago, in order to reduce business overhead, I decided to work from home. I set up a home office. Even now, when I am outside of the office complex, I still utilize a special room in my house as a home office. Working from home can be challenging if you're by yourself. However, when you have children, especially young ones that may constantly be running around it could be even more challenging.

What do you need to do in order to work from home effectively? The answer is divided into the following categories:

1. Your dedicated workspace
2. Your equipment
3. Your personal behavioral attributes
4. People and/or animals around you

First, you need to modify your home/apartment set up in order to dedicate a proper space as your home office. Though many of you may be tempted to work from the kitchen table or while lying on the couch in the living room, I strongly recommend you set up an actual office environment. Choose a room or a corner that can be blocked off or that has a door that you can close and lock. This will allow you to limit disturbances and family members from interfering with your work efforts.

Set up and assign a table as your work desk with a comfortable chair. If you decide to use a computer system, be advised that desktop computers are much more durable than laptops. On the other hand, laptops allow for greater movement flexibility because you can easily transport it and use it almost anywhere. If you choose to work with a laptop make sure to backup all your information at least twice a day, just before lunch and the second time just before you finish your day of work. Make sure you backup information into an external hard drive. I recommend using a solid-state drive that doesn't have any moving components, they are much more dependable. Laptops are not as robust as desktop towers. Therefore, I also recommend getting a laptop cooling fan to dissipate the heat from it to preserve its functionality.

Lighting: the importance of proper lighting could be the difference between you being very productive or stuck and preventing procrastination.

I recommend having three various light systems:

First: Access to natural room light

Second: An adjustable dimmable light

Third: An alternative to sunlight

I personally use all three light systems mentioned, both in my home office as well as in my work office complex. I recommend using this 3 light system because you may experience mood changes. Sometimes the room light may be sufficient, but throughout the day, you may start to feel a bit sluggish or tired. At that point, you can use the adjustable dimmable light to change the rooms light settings to adjust your energy levels.

The third light mentioned is a good source for those working indoors who may not get much sunlight. The alternative sunlight device emits soft white light that usually has two or more settings. It is recommended to use this light at least 15 minutes per day in order to replenish the lack of sunlight and also to help your body metabolize vitamin D better.

Temperature:

It's important to have a suitable temperature in your new home office; if it is too cold or too warm, it will make you uncomfortable and unproductive. During the warm months, you can always use air conditioning or fans. During cold months, I recommend using a regular type heater, not one that works by throwing hot air into the room because they dry the air and may bother your eyes, dry your sinuses, and may make you feel dizzy and cause dehydration. Below is a link for one of the radiators that I have had a good experience with:

Sound:

You may find that wearing earbuds or using headphones may enable you not only to be able to listen to music but also to block out sounds and noises that may disturb you. I recommend using headphones that have a high-quality noise-canceling microphone. In this way, you can communicate remotely with your boss or other workers by using Skype, zoom or any other communication platform.

Your office equipment:
1. A dedicated desk with a comfortable chair
2. A desktop or laptop computers
3. An external solid-state hard drive
4. A printer with extra ink cartridges
5. Printing paper
6. Stationary
7. Shelving system next to your desk [it will prevent clutter]
8. Phone system
9. Reliable high-speed Internet
10. Clock system
11. Project management system

Most of the items listed above do not need further explanation, except the clock and the project management system.

The clock system:

The reason I recommend having a clock is because it is one of the most powerful tools to motivate you and keep you on track. Let's assume you have to create a PowerPoint presentation that has 18 slides. From previous project experience, you know it took you two hours to both write content and design the visual aid slides. If you start working at 9:00 am in the morning, you can give yourself two hours to complete the job. By 11:00 am, you should be done. If you work without a clock to remind you of how long a task actually takes, you may either finish the job sooner or later than desired. Ultimately when your work is not quantified, you are more likely to procrastinate, over/underestimate task time and be less effective.

It may also help to use various alternative alarms systems like the one built into your computer system. It can be set to give you a reminder whenever the alarm or timer is set to go off.

Project management system:

The project management system works hand-in-hand with your clock system. As you gain "work at home" experience and you find out how productive or unproductive you are or can be at home, it is an excellent idea to use a project management system. I will share something I used the project management system for, something many experts told me could not be done by one person, especially not in the time frame I needed it to be done. I took it upon myself to create three vocational school programs that required massive amounts of writing manuals, developing PowerPoint presentations, exams, evaluations, instructor's manuals, shoot and produce professional instructional videos, etc.

I spoke to three consultants who all told me that no man could accomplish what I took upon myself. They told me that in order to write and produce one vocational school program, it should take between half a year to one year with a team of no less than six people working on the program. Not only did I manage to produce 3 programs by myself I also did it in just under 1 ½ yr.

How did I manage to accomplish something that experts said was impossible for one person to do?

I simply used my project management system. I got a huge white dry eraser board and used a permanent marker to divide it into a chart with multiple columns and rows. On the top and at the beginning of each column and row I wrote the topic, date and whatever particular component that needed to be produced and completed. I divided the time into weeks and days. Knowing what I needed to do each week and within each day allow me to know exactly what I had to do in order to be successful. This, by far, was one of the hardest things I've ever done in my life! Sometimes I worked 14 -16 hours days, seven days a week nonstop until the project was done. I recommend you do the same; this is not the only way to manage a project; there are many other excellent project management systems you may find useful.

Refueling yourself:
One of the smartest and gifted Jewish rabbis named the RAMBAM (Rabbi Simón) said:
1. In the morning eat like a king
2. For lunch, eat like a prince
3. For dinner, eat like a vagabond

According to his wisdom, when you are working from home, there is no reason not to eat a great breakfast, as starting fuel for the day. To combat becoming overweight, avoid snacking throughout the day. By having a good breakfast, you will give your body the nutrients it needs to work for longer periods of time. It will not only help to improve your metabolism but also aid in the processing and discarding of toxins that accumulated in your body while you were sleeping.

Physical Exercise:
When you are working from home, think about all the time you are saving, not have to commute back and forth to work. If it's not already a routine for you, I recommend using a fitness system that you can easily perform at home. For those of you who like to walk or run, you could always do it outside. However, if the weather is bad or the neighborhood environment is unsafe, having a treadmill is a great alternative. You could do yoga or Pilates. There are great free videos on YouTube that you can use. In the videos with this book, I included a few

simple physical exercises that you can do in the comfort of your home. You could also use a rope and follow a free tutorial on YouTube on how to do rope jumping for fitness.

Being the CEO of several of my companies, I don't have to show up in the office every day. I could work from home or come to work a little later. I'm grateful for the freedom that I have, but I also want to remind you that I had to work very hard in order to earn this. I hope this will inspire you to take good care of yourself and to be more successful.

Breaks:

It's important to utilize a brake system. What is a brake system? You start your workday with a 50 min work session and 2 x 10min breaks. Then you work 45 minutes and give yourself 2 x 15 min breaks. You can take a lunch break at approx. 12- 1 o'clock. It's very important not to overeat! Ideally, you should leave one-third of your stomach empty. In this way, your digestive system has enough room to produce digestive acids and to move food around. When you overeat, you end up feeling bloated, and the proper digestive process is prevented from happening. All of the food content is not digested, causing inflammation, sickness, feeling tired, and exhausted a few hours after the meal. All of you who do your own laundry in a washing machine knows that if you overstuff a washing machine with clothing, much of the clothes will remain dirty after the wash. You may even end up having to completely stop your washing machine to remove some clothing in order to make some room for the clothes to wash properly. The same thing happens in your stomach. By adopting this one advice, you may find that you not only prevent feeling tired after you eat, but some of your medical problems may start to disappear.

Another special break that I recommend having is a 20 or 30 min nap. In our office, we call it a "power nap." This can be done outside of the 1hr lunch break. Since we started executing "power naps," we've discovered that not only the office staff but also our trainees can stay more focused and energized at 4, 5 and even 6 o'clock in the evening.

Not to overwork:

While you're working from home, it's important to match expectations between your boss and yourself. It is important to set up your daily tasks and your project management system. Once you know that you've completed all your daily tasks, you need to get out of your office and quit your workday. It's important to refresh yourself with various activities that can charge your batteries, like playing with your children, watching TV, playing a video game, going out, etc. If you are the boss, this is an excellent opportunity for you to start to build trustworthy relations with your employees.

Here is an example:

My company filmed a series of active shooter/workplace violence and terrorist attack defense videos for a tactical defense program I created. The processes and equipment we used varied. We used two cameramen, body cameras, eyeglasses cameras, etc. I gave all the footage to one of my video editors to do the editing and post- production. He asked me if he could work from home for the next two weeks so he could work undisturbed. He estimated that he could complete the post-production in this time frame. I allowed him to, and I made sure to check on him every three days. After two weeks, the project was entirely produced and ready for the market.

In another instance, one of my office workers was a very talented combat veteran. One morning I looked at him, and I saw that he was stressed. Empathetically I asked him if he would like to go and work from home for the next few days. He looked at me with disbelief. However, though he was pleased, I told him that he would have to still work on the projects that he was in charge of while at home. After three days, he came back to work, refreshed, fully recharged, and responsibly with the projects that he was in charge of completing.

From my experience, by treating my employees with empathy and wisdom, I got productivity from them that I could not have gotten if I didn't understand human nature, communications, and the importance of rest/recess to rejuvenate the work process and enforce efficiency.

People or animals/pets around you:

It is important to set up rules and mutual boundaries with the other members of the house or the apartment. It could be a family member, your roommate, or uninvited guests, etc. It's essential to set rules, just because you are at home working does not mean that you are available for social interaction all the time. Family members should be reminded to allow you to work quietly. When it comes to young children and toddlers, if you don't have anybody else that can take care of your child while you work, you're going to be a little distracted, but it is doable. Make sure you give them toys, coloring books with markers, etc. to keep them occupied. If you don't have a choice, as a last resort, you can set them up in front of the TV or computer, but then again only as a last resort because this can be destructive long run if you don't predetermine the material they are watching.

CHAPTER 16

STARTING A NEW BUSINESS

If you feel like you have always wanted to start a business, you may have two options:
1. You may already have a business, but because of the Novel Coronavirus world pandemic crisis, you are about to lose it or lose your job potentially.
2. You just graduated from school or some type of training and want to start a new business from scratch.

In both instances, you may find yourself choosing a business that focuses on either a product or service or both. I personally recommend starting a business or modifying your business in a way that you have a combination of both products and services. While there are hundreds of books that teach you how to start your own business, this chapter will share the knowledge that I have accumulated from being in business for the past 20 years after starting with just $90. First, you need to create a product or service wheel.

For example: if you want to manufacture perfume for women, this is your product.

In your product wheel, you could place additional products or services. A women's perfume business has many potential additional products, sub-products, as well as services and sub-services that you can add, such as women's sunglasses, scarf, hats, hair, and nail products, soaps, natural oils and scents, candles, fashionable umbrellas, etc. As for services, for a women's perfume business, you could broker and network with hair salons and beauty parlors around the city, state, or even internationally. Not only selling the perfume retail/wholesale, but also via an incentivized or commission-based referral program to increase revenue streams. Secondly, you need to choose a business that has very low overhead; the lower your overhead is (initial product cost/expenses), the more profit you will generate. Another example is a joint venture broker business, which usually has very low overhead.

I want to give you another example of how you can do business with low overhead and be very successful. And this is cyberspace, artificial intelligence, and the software field, which is one of the most profitable businesses to have.

First, you need to educate yourself and then contact various dedicated freelancers that qualify to work for/with you remotely. You should network around program developers, apps builders and designers, AI implementation and software developers, software functionality testers, web development, business plan writers, legal support, etc. I'm hoping you get the picture. Secondly, you should be the project manager for each project. You can hire someone to do it, or you can learn to be able to estimate task completion time and calculate the potential cost to complete the project. As long as you have a good team around you and you can meet deadlines, you can start a business like the one I just described. Nowadays, this can all be made possible by just sending a few emails, arranging and signing some mutual contracts with some freelancers, creating a website and a brand. In most first- world countries, to run a business, you have to be legit; this is why you should inquire about what kind of permits or licenses you should have or get before launching your business. Make sure you're in complete compliance with all state, city, and county legal authorities and that you are complying with all applicable regulations.

The next phase is your marketing and sales. In today's day and age, if you are not visible online and on social media, you practically don't exist. Without visibility, there is no public awareness. Therefore, you must develop a marketing plan and try to execute it effectively. It's good to advertise and post on the main social media platforms such as Facebook, Instagram, Pinterest, LinkedIn, Google, and YouTube. As a matter of fact, do some prior research to determine which social media/media platforms are best for your business type. Make or have somebody else make a website for you and learn how to maintain it yourself. From experience, you can make any changes you want/need in just a few minutes; this makes progress very convenient.

I'll give you an example: During the war on terrorism, I was running a counter-terrorism training school, and someone sent me a video that showed executions and the beheadings of some terrorist victims. I remember it was 10 o'clock at night, as soon as I saw the videos, I went to my home office, wrote down a new web page idea titled "escaping from captivity and execution attempt survival course." Within two weeks, we got bombarded with interest from both corporate companies and government agencies. This course not only helps to save many lives; it also made quite a bit of profit as well. It is also good to go to trade shows and conferences to learn more about your industry, get ideas, and, most importantly, to network, market and sell your products and/or services.

Now, what if you already have a business, or if you had to let go of some or all of your employees, and you're wondering how you can bounce back. In this situation I recommend, if you have a brick-and-mortar type of business to think about which businesses or products fit your business wheel. Then place an ad and find businesses that are in the same situation that could use some of your business products or even your store space. For example, you have a barbershop, and your business suffered because of the Novel Coronavirus crisis. You can always get additional chairs and hire additional barbers; this is naturally the smart thing to do. Also, if you have additional space you can share, you could get creative and get someone to work that space to generate more revenue. I.e., get a massage therapist that has his/her own table and section it off with dividers, curtains, or more permanent walls. At that point, you could rent to the massage therapist or, instead, get 20- 25% of what they make.

You could also find businesses, real estate agents, insurance agents, etc. that would like to advertise to your customers. You could place a flat-screen TV and run commercials for those who are interested and charge them a commission and/or a fee. These are some simple examples of how you could leverage your space and increase your revenue. Different businesses may have to do different things in order to leverage their available space and resources.

Another business idea is to buy into a franchise. You could purchase franchises from $10,000 all the way to several hundreds of thousands, if not millions of dollars. The good thing about franchises is that you can talk to other franchise owners, attend training or potentially educate yourself and get a feel of the business to see if you are passionate about it while to be applying for the funds needed to buy into the franchise.

Word of caution; be especially careful with buying brand new franchises since there is a lack of a proven track record of reliable success history for you to base your buying decision off of. As a veteran entrepreneur, I offer consultation and training to both individuals and corporations on how to start or improve businesses, how to create better opportunities, and much more.

Those who are interested can take a look at the end of this book to find out how to contact my team and me.

CHAPTER 17

THE DEEP SIDE OF MARKETING THAT MANY DON'T KNOW

In previous chapters, I included this information in this book because, unfortunately, the Coronavirus world pandemic has had such a devastating effect on our modern civilization that I feel many of you reading this book want to bounce back and restore our civilization as it was or even better.

When I talk about the deep side of marketing, it is something I had to investigate for myself. Though I hired various marketing experts and companies and spent thousands of dollars, I still didn't see a good return on my investment.

Only after I investigated deeply did I realize why many marketing companies were failing me and how to do the proper marketing for one of my businesses, which is a vocational school.

What I found out was that I needed to define, in the clearest manner possible, who was the ideal client for each one of my vocational school programs. There I discovered the term customer persona or ideal client. However, what was the norm did not satisfy me because I felt there were missing components. I divided my approach to resolving this challenge to determining my school's ideal customer persona and increasing business by analyzing our customers in the following ways, emotionally, mentally, physically, spiritually, monetarily, and according to their location.

Then I developed a marketing strategy according to the customer data we collected over the last several years. I noticed that there were some obvious differences and common traits within our school's customers. When I finished, I had a chart that helped me to determine the differences between each ideal customer for each program I offered at my vocational school.

Next, I developed several scripts for a few appealing promo videos based on the information I was able to determine about whom our ideal customers were and what they wanted. Then my team and I narrated and produced the videos

As you can see below, here are the links for the strategic videos that were produced according to the process that I described above.

ADVANCED BODYGUARD/PSD OPERATOR COURSE

https://youtu.be/8rLMl-2JFAg

KRAV HAGANAH INSTRUCTOR

https://youtu.be/0gMbjFYmEUE

COUNTER-TERRORISM INSTRUCTOR

https://youtu.be/apKMVrtvV44

I strongly recommend you click on each link individually to see for yourself the extremely appealing professional videos we produced that were the outcome of the above insightful marketing process.

If you implement the process that has been described here to your type of service business or products business your marketing campaign could get amazing results.

For consultation on how to incorporate this process into your business or career you may contact us directly using the information at the end of this book.

CHAPTER 18

DIGITAL MARKETER PROFESSION

Another extremely beneficial modern and beneficial profession is the digitalmarketer certification from Ryan Deiss company, DigitalMarketer.com. It is my opinion that Ryan and his team have created the most advanced digital marketing training program in the world. They have a fantastic portal full of online training programs, certification programs, guides books, labs, coaching, and many other self-learning tools.

I have a good friend of mine that, after taking digitalmarketer training certification programs, became one of the top online and offline marketers in the world today. Using the skill sets he's learned through DigitalMarketer's training, he's been able to create and manage marketing campaigns that have generated hundreds of thousands of dollars on a monthly basis for various clients.

During these uncertain economic times, DigitalMarketer's products and certifications programs have positively changed the lives of so many who've been impacted by the coronavirus.

I strongly recommend you to check their website: https://www.digitalmarketer.com and find out how you can acquire, improve, and advance yourself or your business in the field of digital marketing.

If you have any questions about the DigitalMarketer program and how it can help change people's lives, you may contact Enrique Marin at enrique@armingpatriots.com

CHAPTER 19

MEDICAL RESCUE BY THE AUTHOR AT 30,000 FEET

This event happened several years ago. I remember the tension on the passenger's faces and the heightened energy in the air. While we were boarding the plane, I could sense the distress, would a missile shoot down our flight? As I took my seat in the business class in the front of the plane, I could see the worrying faces of the passengers as they were passing by me on the way to store the carry-on luggage and take their seats. It was well past midnight, and the flight was preparing to depart to Europe with the flight path passing over hostile terrorist territories.

While the plane took off, everything was dark around the aircraft and the runway. I had never seen a plane take off with no lights, so I guessed the flight crew was concerned about missiles as well.

We were two hours into the flight, and suddenly a scream was heard throughout the plane. It was a woman screaming in pain; the sound was coming from the very back of the aircraft. The flight attendant quickly rushed to the woman to see what was wrong, and after a few minutes, the flight attendants brought the woman to the front of the plane. The flight attendants had laid the woman down on the plane floor right across from my seat. The woman was screaming with all of her might;

obviously, she was in tremendous pain; she was grabbing her stomach, screaming, and crying. Thru the dim cabin lights, I could see the worried faces of the flight attendant as they were asking if there were any doctors on the plane, anyone who could help, a nurse, maybe a paramedic. When the flight attendant heard no reply, she then pleaded, is there anybody here with any medical experience? All we heard was an eerie silence; no one talked. Everyone was silent, so the only noise was the woman on the floor crying and the sound of the jet engines soaring through the sky. I looked back to see if anyone was approaching. It was evident that there was nobody on the plane that could render aid and help this poor woman. So I contacted the flight attendants and told her, "I'm not a doctor; neither I am a nurse or a paramedic; however, I have some medical knowledge."

When I was a child, I had dreamed of becoming a doctor, so I read several of the medical diagnostic books that I could get my hands on and also the Encyclopedia. I never in a million years thought would I ever need to put this basic information to use. When I approached the woman, she was extremely pale. I remember thinking to myself; "there are a thousand things that can be wrong with this woman, what is it that is causing this horrendous pain?"

I asked her to sit down on the floor and checked her eyes with a small flashlight that I had with me. I was looking to see signs of internal bleeding or grayish or yellowish color, but her eyes were watery and clean. I was happy, no internal bleeding or head injury. I checked her pulse on both of her wrists and her neck. Her pulse was irregular sometimes fast and sometimes a little slow, so I asked her what's wrong with you, where does it hurt? She pointed to her stomach, actually the right side of her stomach. I asked her if she had an accident, maybe she had eaten something bad? When the last time that she had to urinate? Did she see any blood when she urinated? She said, "no blood." I thought to myself great; I think I know what's wrong with her. Her appendicitis was causing the pain, but I did not believe that it had burst. I decided to check, so I asked her to let go of her stomach, then I pressed my fingers on the right side of her stomach, and I asked her does it hurts. She replied no, then I let go slowly and asked her, does it hurts now? She replied no again, so I tried again. I pressed back on the right side of her waist, and I asked, does it hurt? She said no, so I very rapidly and surprisingly released the pressure. She immediately screamed and jumped in the air. I was convinced that she defiantly had a problem with her appendicitis. I was still convinced that it had not burst, so I immediately asked the flight attendants to help me. They brought me some blankets, pillows, and a bag of ice. I made the woman as comfortable as possible with the blankets and pillows, and then I asked the woman to breathe in a specific manner. I wanted her to breathe in slowly, pause, and then exhale. I wanted to hypnotize her. I have had many years of education in transpersonal psychology when I was living in the state of Israel in Israel. All of my studies were becoming very useful, as I guided her through the hypnosis. When she grew calmer, I laid the bag of ice on the right side of her stomach to cool down the area.

As the hypnosis progressed, the pained expression on her face starts to vanish. After about twenty-five minutes, she was calm and relaxed. I sat next to her on the plane floor and monitored her every few minutes until the plane landed. As the plane finally landed, I could see an EMS vehicle rush toward us. The plane door opened, and a paramedic team climbed up and rushed toward the woman. I told them what I had done and thought. The paramedic conducted the same check that I performed and agreed with my assessment. The two flight attendants approached me and shook my hand , hugged me, and each kissed me on my cheek. They said, thank you for helping us in saving the life of this woman. I smiled; I was happy. I was glad I was able to stabilize her until she could get real medical care. Years later, I shared the story with a medical surgeon friend of mine. He said he would've done the same things if he was on that flight. He thought the hypnosis was a great idea.

This event was the second time that I diagnosed appendicitis illness; when I was 12 years old, my mom complained about pain in her stomach, so my dad and I took her to the hospital to the ER, their doctor that checked her told her she has nothing serious. And that she should go back home, as my father went to get the car I ran after him and I told him, please not to take mom back home. I think she has an appendicitis issue, my father replied, Doron, didn't you hear the doctor? I replied to him I believe that the doctor is very wrong so my father went back to the ER and talk to the head nurse, the head nurse told my father to wait and that in half an hour another doctor will come and that she will ask the new doctor to check my mom. Indeed, after half an hour, another doctor entered, and immediately the nurse took him to see my mom. After a minute check, he rushed the medical staff to take my mom to the operating room for an appendicitis surgery immediately; a few days later, my mom was released back home.

CHAPTER 20

BOOK CONCLUSION, OPPORTUNITIES & RESOURCES

As you may already know after reading this book the coronavirus epidemic is one of the worst crises the world has ever known since the second world war. Almost every country in the world are facing the same problems and challenges. The main two problems that I see that have to be addressed are the vulnerabilities of the elder population and those who have pre-existing illnesses and the economic crisis which carries much more gravity for billions of people all over the globe.

Fear of the novel Covid 19 urges governments to shut down their country's economies without any discrimination. This cause of action has had a catastrophic effect on many companies, businesses, workers and employees.

In my opinion, the economic crisis should be addressed now while simultaneously doctors and scientists try to produce a vaccine and medicine.

This book and video program that we have created are two tools that can educate many people about preventative steps they can take to help stay safe and potentially adjust their working situation accordingly during this health and economic pandemic.

On the economic and crisis recovery section of this book, though there is much knowledge and tips, I feel I barely touched the topic for the situation is evolving and changing every day. There is so much involved in the total scope of this topic, what I wrote is almost like an effective first aid treatment verses a massive in depth analysis and address.

Many individuals and organizations are going to need out-of-the-box solutions; you can find more about my company and my consultation services, public speaking and custom training program design and delivery.

Thank you for investing in my book, may you and your loved ones remain safe and prosper!

Doron Benbenisty

On behalf of my company and I, consultation services are available for the following:

Large, medium and small organizations, governments, both city states and countries, head of countries, fortune 500 companies, airlines, cruise lines, train and subway organizations and companies, casino resorts, hotels, government agencies both in the US and international, US military, friendly to the US foreign military and many more organizations, entities and individuals.

Our Services:

1. Consultations provided both online and in person.
2. Licensing and Sales of our Coronavirus and Infectious Diseases Defense Online Program.
3. Custom Training Program Design and Creation are available.
4. Advisor to Businesses or the Self-Employed if in need of reinventing itself.
5. Protocol Development and Compliance Policy Development.
6. Licensing The Covid 19 and Infectious Diseases Online Video Program.
7. Licensing The Covid 19, Infectious Diseases Defense and Economic Recovery Book.
8. Public Speaking.
9. Strategic and Tactical Sales and Marketing Asset Creation.
10. Coaching with Doron.
11. Advisory by Doron.
12. Mastermind with Doron.
13. Curriculum Development [Ghost Writing].
14. Problem Solving and Solution Finding.

Additional products that have been created and developed by Doron for sale:

1. The Covid 19 and Infectious Diseases Defense Video Program
2. The Covid 19, Infectious Diseases Defense and Economic Crisis Recovery Book
3. Active Shooter, Workplace Violence and Terrorist Attack Online Video Program
4. Home Invasion Survival Book
5. Home/Business Owner Protection Program
6. Doron Defensive Tactic System
7. How To Defeat A Bully Book
8. Tactical Folding Knife Video

Educational training programs that were developed by Doron and are available for licensing and/or partnerships:

1. Professional Drone Pilot Course – 15 Days
2. Tactical Drone Pilot Course - 15 Days
3. 20 Tactical Drone Courses – 5 Days each
4. Public Safety Drone Pilot Course - 16 Weeks
5. Bodyguard/PSD Operator Course- 15 Days
6. Counter Terrorism Instructor Course - 20 Days
7. Krav Haganah Instructor/Defensive Tactics Instructor Course- 15 Days
8. 5 X Law Enforcement Post Courses
9. Counter Terrorism Operator Course - 15 Days
10. Executive Protection Operative Course – 7 Days
11. Professional Tactical Driver Course - 15 Day
12. Digital Marketing Specialist Course - 15 Day

Doron's inventions and innovations investment opportunities:

1. Tactical Drone Interceptor
2. Dr. On Demand
3. Nightmares – PTSD/TBI/TRAUMA Eliminator
4. Counter Carjacking/Kidnapping Vehicle System
5. Counter Vehicle Booby Trapping System
6. Vegas Tactical Adventures Attraction Project
7. Drone Marketing and Drone Fare Entertainment Project

Contact information for our services

cri@critraining.com

Phone: 702 – 222 – 3489

CRI TRAINING and CRI INSTITUTE DIVISION

www.critraining.com

www.ingramcontent.com/pod-product-compliance
Lightning Source LLC
Chambersburg PA
CBHW071420210526
45465CB00001B/471